Discover

BRIAN ABBS · INGRID FREEBAIRN

STUDENTS' BOOK 3

Longman

Contents

LANGUAGE USE   LANGUAGE

Someone I admire.

MERYL STREEP

PRINCESS ANNE

BOB GELDOF

Look!

Someone I admire very much is ...
The subjects he likes best are ...

Andy Morgan

Andy Morgan is a fourteen-year-old English boy who lives in Dover. He goes to school at Castle Hill Secondary School where he is in his third year. The subjects he likes best at school are Geography and Computer Studies. He is taking his 'O' level examinations in two years' time. When he leaves school he would like to travel round the world for a year. In his spare time he likes cycling and playing chess and he is learning to play the guitar. Someone he admires very much is Bob Geldof, a man who helped to raise a lot of money for famine relief.

---

1 **In pairs, ask and answer questions to complete the chart for Andy.**

1. What's his name?
2. How old is he?
3. What nationality is he?
4. Where does he live?
5. Where does he go to school and what year is he in?
6. Which subjects does he like best?
7. What are his next important examinations?
8. What would he like to do when he leaves school?
9. What does he like doing in his spare time?
10. Is there someone special he admires?

Name: *Andy Morgan*
Age:
Nationality:
Home town:
School and year:
Next examinations:
Favourite subjects:
Ambition:
Hobbies and interests:
Someone he admires:

SADE

CHRIS HALLAM: A COMPETITOR IN THE LONDON MARATHON

WINNIE MANDELA AND BISHOP TUTU

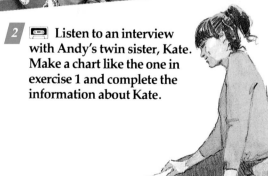

2 🔲 Listen to an interview with Andy's twin sister, Kate. Make a chart like the one in exercise 1 and complete the information about Kate.

3 Use the chart to interview someone in your class.

4 Write sentences about people and things you like or don't like.

A film star I like/admire very much is …
A TV programme I don't like/hate is …

a film or TV star	a book
a pop star	a film
a sports personality	a TV programme
a politician	a school subject

5 Use the notes and the paragraph about Andy to write about Andy's penfriend in Hong Kong.

Name:	Vicki Wong
Age:	15
Nationality:	Chinese
School and year:	Hamilton High School Hong Kong (4th year)
Next examinations:	'O' levels
Favourite subjects:	English and History
Ambition:	To go to France and learn fashion design
Hobbies and interests:	Music, disco dancing and reading English poetry
Someone she admires:	Princess Anne

6 Write a penfriend letter to Vicki telling her about yourself. Begin your letter like this:

*Your address
Date*

Dear Vicki,
　　　　My name is …

End your letter:
　　　　Yours sincerely,
　　　　(Your name)

I'll carry it.

■ Dialogue

Kate and Andy Morgan are saying goodbye to their American cousin, Cindy. Kate's friend, Sue, is also at the Morgans' house.

MRS MORGAN: Kate! Andy! Cindy's leaving in a few minutes. Come and say goodbye.
SUE: Where are you going, Cindy?
CINDY: I'm going to travel round Europe for a couple of months.
KATE: You are lucky!
CINDY: Ah, there's Rick! He's taking me to the station.
RICK: Hi everybody!
ANDY: Shall I take your rucksack for you?
CINDY: Thanks, Andy, but you needn't bother. I'll carry it.
RICK: OK. Let's go.
CINDY: Bye, everyone! I'll send you a postcard!

1 Which is correct?

1. Cindy is going
   a) to the USA.
   b) to Europe.

2. She is starting her journey
   a) by train.
   b) by plane.

3. Rick is taking Cindy
   a) to Paris.
   b) to the station.

4. Rick
   a) has not met Kate and Andy before.
   b) knows Kate and Andy.

2 Match the situations with the correct responses.

1. You are leaving school on Friday afternoon.
2. Someone phones your mother but she is out.
3. You are going on a trip.
4. You are finishing a letter to a friend.
5. You telephone a friend who is busy.

I'll phone back later.
I'll see you on Monday.
I'll write again soon.
I'll tell her you phoned.
I'll send you a postcard.

3 In pairs, offer to do things. Accept or refuse the offer.

A: I'll make some tea./Shall I make some tea?
B: Thanks, that's very kind of you./Thanks, but you needn't bother. I'll do it.

Offer to:
   make some tea or coffee.
   make some sandwiches.
   call for your friend tomorrow morning.
   walk home with your friend .

4 Write a dialogue. You are going to Britain for your summer holidays. You go round to a friend's house to say goodbye.

Your friend asks you where you are going.
You reply and say you will send a postcard.
Your friend says thank you.
You say you'll see your friend next term.
Your friend says goodbye.

I've been to Britain.

Personal Experience Chart

Name: *Vicki Wong*

E X P E R I E N C E S

Foreign Travel

Have you ever been to a foreign country? *Yes*

Which one(s)? *Singapore and Britain*

When did you go? *Singapore - at Christmas*
Britain - last summer

Sports Events

Have you ever been to a big sports event? *Yes*

What sort? *A tennis tournament (Wimbledon)*

Accidents

Have you ever broken any bones? *Yes*

What did you break? *My arm*

How did you break it? *I fell off a horse.*

Look!
Have you ever been to Britain?
I've been to Britain twice.
I've never been to France.

---

1 Ask and answer about Vicki's experiences.

A: Has she ever been to a foreign country?
B: Yes, she has. She's been to Singapore and Britain.
A: When did she go?
B: She went to Singapore at Christmas and she went to Britain last summer.

2 In pairs, ask and answer about your experiences.

A: Have you ever been to Britain/a big sports event?
B: Yes, I have./Yes, I've been to …
or
No, I haven't./No, I've never been to …

---

3 Look at part of one of Vicki's letters to Andy. Write a paragraph to your penfriend. Use the experiences you talked about in exercise 2.

2) I've never been to the USA but I have been to Britain once. I went last summer and I watched the tennis at Wimbledon. I saw Gabriela Sabatini and Boris Becker. It was wonderful. Have you ever been to Wimbledon?

Did you know?

Nine tonnes of strawberries are eaten during the two weeks of the Wimbledon Championships.

Hitch-hiking

Read and answer.
Is hitch-hiking only dangerous for hitch-hikers?
Is hitch-hiking allowed in all countries?

Hitch-hiking was once a cheap and friendly way
to travel but nowadays it is quite dangerous. You
often hear stories of hitch-hikers who are
attacked or murdered by drivers, or of drivers
who are robbed by hitch-hikers. Because of this,
hitch-hiking is not allowed in many countries.

Danny, 15, a schoolboy

"I live in the country. I
often hitch-hike into town
to save money. I always
get lifts from people I
know but sometimes I
have to wait quite a long
time."

Paul, 20, a student

"I've hitch-hiked for three
years. I've been all over
Europe. I enjoy it. You
meet a lot of people. You
should look friendly and
maybe a little scruffy – but
not too scruffy!"

Susan, 42, a housewife

'I don't like it. I think it's dangerous. None of my children are allowed to do it. I prefer to buy them a train ticket rather than let them hitch-hike.'

Kerry, 19, a nurse

'I've hitch-hiked since I was sixteen. I don't go alone. I go with my boyfriend or a girlfriend. My mum hates it but I've never had any bad experiences. I know how to look after myself.'

Look!

How long have you hitch-hiked?

I've hitch-hiked	since I was 16.
	since 1986.
	for two years.

1 **Answer about each person.**

1. Danny
Where does he live?
Why does he hitch-hike?
Does he always get a lift at once?

2. Paul
How long has he hitch-hiked?
Where has he been?
Does he like it? Why?
What does he think a hitch-hiker should look like?

3. Susan
What does she think of hitch-hiking?
Do her children hitch-hike?
What does she prefer to do?

4. Kerry
How long has she hitch-hiked?
Does she hitch-hike alone?
What does her mother think of it?
Has she ever had any bad experiences?

2 **In pairs, ask and answer these questions.**

1. How long have you been at your school?
2. How long have you lived in your present home?
3. How long have you known your best friend?
4. How long have you studied English?

3 **Write some sentences about someone in your family, using** since **or** for.

4 📼 **Listen to Jo talking about hitch-hiking. Note the arguments for and against hitch-hiking.**

5 **Roleplay a situation in which a parent forbids a 16-year-old to go on a hitch-hiking holiday with a friend. Use your notes from exercise 4.**

Roleplay

By chance Kate meets one of her cousins, Josh, as he gets off the hovercraft in Dover. In pairs, use the guide to act out their conversation.

KATE   JOSH

Say hello and ask what Josh is doing in Dover.

Say you have been on holiday in France.

Ask how long he was there.

Say how long. Ask Kate if she's ever been to France.

Say you went there last summer.

Say you are going to hitch-hike to London now.

Say you hope he gets a lift. Say goodbye.

Say goodbye. Say you'll send a postcard from London.

Now write the conversation.

Listen

'Guess who? Guess what?'
Listen to this radio quiz and see if you can guess the person before the panel. There are ten questions.

Write

Your uncle has given you a present for passing your exams. Use this guide to write him a 'thank you' letter.

Your address
Date

Dear Uncle …,

Paragraph 1
Thank him for the present and say why you like it or how often you use it.

Paragraph 2
Tell him some of the things you did last year at school.

Paragraph 3
Say how long you've been on holiday and say when you'll come and see him.

End your letter:
Love from,
(Your name)

Dictionary skills

Put these words into alphabetical order.

summer	subject	school
station	song	student
send	star	
see	sport	

Grammar Lessons 1-5

Present simple

Andy Morgan	lives goes to school	in Dover.

Present continuous as future

He	is	taking his 'O' level exams	in two years' time.
She		doing her exams	next summer.

Defining relative clauses with who

Andy	is	an English boy	who	lives in Dover.
Bob Geldof		a man		helped to raise money for famine relief.

Non-defining relative clause with where

He	goes to Castle Hill School	where	he	is in	his	third year.
She			she		her	

Contact clauses

Someone	(whom)	he admires	very much is	Bob Geldof.
A film star		I like		Matt Dillon.

The subjects	(which)	he likes best are French and Maths.
A TV programme		I hate is 'Dallas'.

Simple future (promises)

I'll	send you a postcard. write again soon.

Modal Shall I'll *(offers)*

Shall I	carry it make some tea	for you?

I'll	carry it make some tea	for you.

Modal needn't

You needn't bother.

Past simple

When did	you she	go?

I	went	last summer.
She		to Singapore at Christmas.

Present perfect

Have you ever been to	Britain? Wimbledon?

Yes,	I	have.	I've	been to Britain twice.
No,		haven't.		never been to France.

Present perfect with since *and* for

How long have you hitch-hiked?

I've hitch-hiked	since	I was 16. 1986.
	for two years.	

I've already found a job.

🖭 Dialogue

Tony Mills is the director of a small London company called AIP (Anything Is Possible) which does all sorts of jobs from cleaning houses to finding a hippopotamus for a party! AIP has just opened a new office in Canterbury, a large city in Kent. Tony is very busy and is looking for more staff to help him.

RICK: Hello.

TONY: Hello! Is that Rick Hunter?

RICK: Speaking.

TONY: Hi, My name's Tony Mills from AIP. Cindy Farrow gave me your number. She worked for us this summer.

RICK: I know. She's just gone to Europe.

TONY: That's right. Well, we need some extra help and she gave me your number.

RICK: I've already found a part-time job, I'm afraid.

TONY: That's a shame. We want someone to start next Saturday at the Balloon Festival.

RICK: Balloon Festival? Oh well, the other job was only at the petrol station and I haven't started yet. Perhaps I could work for you instead.

TONY: OK. Come to our office in Canterbury and we'll talk about it.

1 Which is correct?

1. a) Cindy Farrow is still working for AIP.
   b) Cindy Farrow has finished working for AIP.

2. a) AIP has an office only in London.
   b) AIP has offices in London and Canterbury.

3. a) Tony Mills knows Rick Hunter well.
   b) Tony Mills has never met Rick Hunter.

4. a) Rick already has a job.
   b) Rick has no job for the summer.

5. a) Tony offers Rick a job at AIP.
   b) Tony offers him a job at a petrol station.

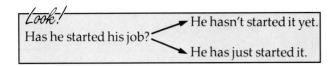

Look!

Has he started his job? ⟶ He hasn't started it yet.
⟶ He has just started it.

2 **Look at the pictures and answer the questions.**

1. Has she finished her homework?
   No, she hasn't finished it yet.
   (She's still doing it.)

2. Has he arrived at the station?

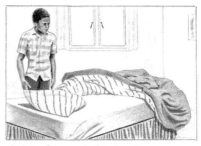

3. Has he made his bed?

4. Has she had breakfast?

5. Has she seen *The Man from Mars*?

6. Has he done the washing-up?

Look!

I've already found a job.

3 **Complete this conversation with a friend. You have already done everything your friend wants you to do.**

FRIEND: Do you want to read this magazine?
YOU: (No, thanks, I've already read it.)
FRIEND: I've just bought The Cars latest album. Do you want to hear it?
YOU: ....
FRIEND: Well, what shall we do then? Shall we go to see *Ghostbusters III*?
YOU: ....
FRIEND: What about having a Coke then?
YOU:
FRIEND: Well, I'm going to have one. And then let's do our homework together.
YOU: ....
FRIEND: You are a pain!

4 **Write a dialogue. You are on a train. The ticket inspector arrives.**

The inspector asks for your ticket.
You say you have lost it.
The inspector asks you to buy another one.
You say you haven't got any money.
The inspector asks why.
You say you have lost your purse as well!

Take the M20 to Maidstone.

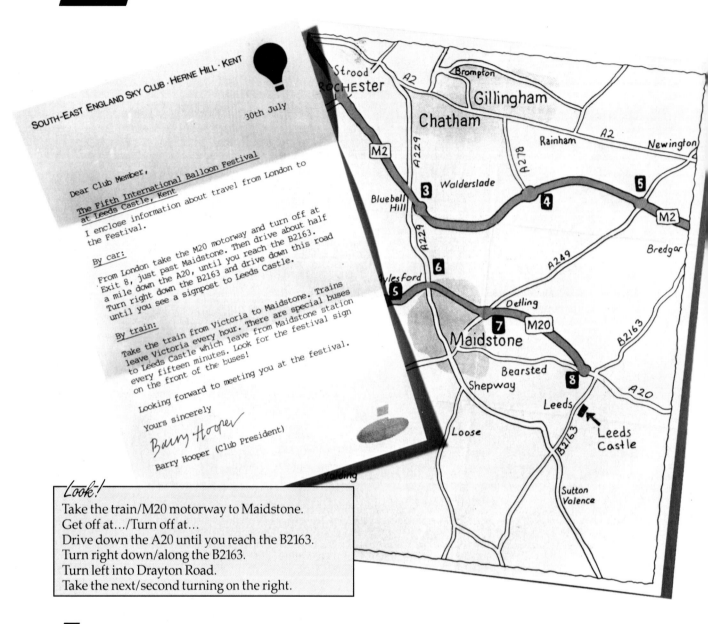

SOUTH-EAST ENGLAND SKY CLUB · HERNE HILL · KENT

30th July

Dear Club Member,

The Fifth International Balloon Festival
at Leeds Castle, Kent

I enclose information about travel from London to
the Festival.

By car:

From London take the M20 motorway and turn off at
Exit 8, just past Maidstone. Then drive about half
a mile down the A20, until you reach the B2163.
Turn right down the B2163 and drive down this road
until you see a signpost to Leeds Castle.

By train:

Take the train from Victoria to Maidstone. Trains
leave Victoria every hour. There are special buses
to Leeds Castle which leave from Maidstone station
every fifteen minutes. Look for the festival sign
on the front of the buses!

Looking forward to meeting you at the festival.

Yours sincerely

Barry Hooper

Barry Hooper (Club President)

Look!

Take the train/M20 motorway to Maidstone.
Get off at…/Turn off at…
Drive down the A20 until you reach the B2163.
Turn right down/along the B2163.
Turn left into Drayton Road.
Take the next/second turning on the right.

---

1 📼 **Complete the telephone conversation with Rick. Use the information in the letter.**

RICK: Can I go all the way to Leeds Castle by train?
YOU: ……… .
RICK: What do I do when I get off at Maidstone?
YOU: ……… .
RICK: How often do the buses leave?
YOU: ……… .
RICK: Mmm. Maybe I'll go by motorbike. I know I have to take the M20 but when do I turn off?
YOU: ……… .
RICK: Yes, and then what?
YOU: ……… .
RICK: Hold on! I want to write that down. Turn left down the B2163. Is that right?
YOU: ……… .
RICK: OK. Thanks. I'll see you there. Bye!

2 📼 **Listen to Rick giving directions to a friend. As you listen, follow the route from Maidstone and name the town to which he is directing his friend.**

3 **Write a note to a friend. Explain how to get to your school by train or underground from the main railway station. Say how long the journey takes. Say if you have to change trains or take some other means of transport, e.g. tram or bus.**

Did you know?

'Ham' and 'Sandwich' are real places in Kent in England. There is a place called 'Banana' in Australia.

Around the world in 80 days

🔲 Read and listen

It is the year 1872, Phileas Fogg has just had lunch with some friends at his club in London.

The six men sat down at a table and began to play cards. Stuart spoke after the game.
'The world's not very big,' he said. 'We can go round it now in three months.'
5 'In eighty days only,' said Phileas Fogg.
'You can't do it in eighty days,' replied Stuart.
'I can,' said Fogg. 'How much do you want to bet?'
'Four thousand pounds,' Stuart said.
10 'Only four thousand?' Fogg continued. 'I have twenty thousand in the bank. I'll bet all of it.'
'Twenty thousand?' Stuart asked in amazement.

'I won't lose,' said Fogg. 'Eighty days is quite
15 enough for me. But you must bet me twenty thousand pounds too. Do you accept?'
The five men talked together and then answered him. 'We accept,' they said. 'When do you begin the journey?'
20 'There's a train to Dover at a quarter to nine. I'll take it.'
'This evening?'
'Yes, this evening,' Fogg answered.
'Today is October 2nd. I'll be back on
25 December 21st at a quarter to nine. And now, let's play a game of cards. Begin please, Mr Stuart.'

1 **Which is correct?**

1. Fogg says he can travel round the world in
   a) three months.
   b) less than three months.

2. His friends bet
   a) £20,000 altogether
   b) £4,000 altogether
   that he can't do the journey in that time.

3. He decides to do the journey because
   a) he wants to win the bet.
   b) he already has a train ticket.

4. Fogg decides to leave
   a) on December 21st.
   b) the same evening.

2 **Copy the correct sentences from exercise 1 to make a summary.**

3 **Look at the text and find the past tenses of these verbs.**

say	continue	answer	reply
ask	speak	talk	begin

Joke time!

MAN: A return ticket, please.
RAILWAY CLERK: Where to?
MAN: Back here, of course!

Up, up and away!

Read and answer.

When did the first hot-air balloon take off?

Who were its first passengers?

Have you ever wanted to fly like a bird? Well, one way of getting off the ground without wings is in a balloon. At the end of the eighteenth century, the Montgolfier brothers from France discovered that hot air can lift a balloon. In 1783 the first hot-air balloon took off with its first passengers – a duck, a chicken and a sheep! Today thousands of people enjoy ballooning as a hobby.

1 **True or False?**

1. The Montgolfier brothers were French.
2. They lived at the beginning of this century.
3. They found out how to make a balloon lift into the air.
4. They flew in the first hot-air balloon.

HOW DO BALLOONS FLY?

A hot-air balloon floats because hot air is lighter than cool air. A hot-air balloon consists of a basket in which the pilot and the crew stand, a gas burner and a large balloon. To take off, you turn on the burner which heats the air inside the balloon. When the air gets hot, the balloon rises. To land, you allow the air inside the balloon to cool.

Alison says:
'I went ballooning once but I prefer gliding. It's great! I started last year and quite honestly, it's the most exciting thing I've ever done. It's much more fun than flying an aeroplane or a balloon. Gliding gives me a terrific feeling of freedom but it's sometimes quite frightening when the wind is strong.'

Look!

I enjoy gliding.
Gliding is much more fun than ballooning.

---

3 Match the words in the three columns to make sensible sentences.

1. Travelling by air is much faster than travelling by train.

1. Travelling by air	much worse		writing English.
2. Windsurfing	much more dangerous		travelling by train.
3. Speaking English	is much more expensive	than	water skiing.
4. Hang-gliding	much faster		skating.
5. Skiing	much more difficult		feeling sick.
6. Having a cold	much more fun		ballooning.

4 In pairs, discuss your comparisons.

A: Having a cold is much worse than feeling sick.
B: I agree./I don't agree. I think it's the opposite.

Joke time!
Robert was lost in a hot-air balloon somewhere over Scotland. As he passed over a farm he called to a farmer. 'Hello there! Where am I?'
The farmer looked up. 'You can't fool me!' he shouted. 'You're up there in that little basket!'

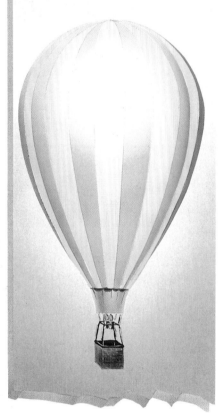

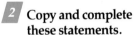

2 Copy and complete these statements.

1. A balloon floats because …
2. The basket underneath the balloon is where …
3. As well as a balloon and a basket, you need …
4. When you turn on the burner, the air inside the balloon … and the balloon …
5. When you want to land, you must allow …

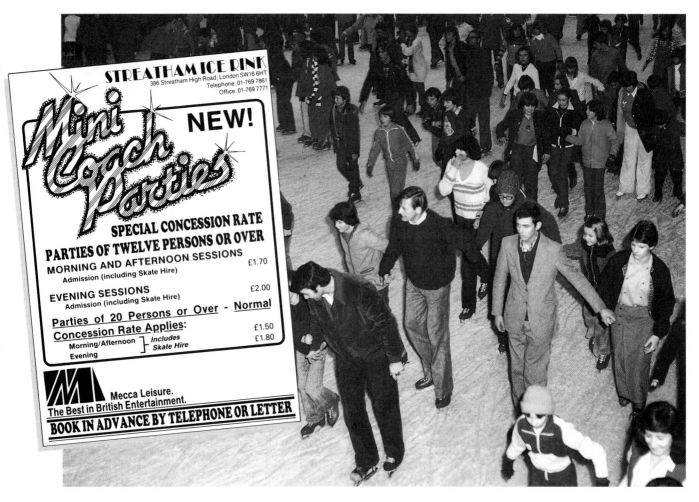

Roleplay

Roleplay this telephone conversation with a friend.

YOU | FRIEND

> Ask if your friend has received your letter.

> > Say it hasn't arrived yet.

> Say you want him/her to come ice skating with you next Saturday.

> > Ask how much it costs and what time you should arrive.

> Give the information.

> > Accept the invitation and say you'll come by train. Ask how to get there.

> Give directions to your house from the station.

Now write your conversation.

Write

Write a paragraph about why you like your favourite sport or hobby. Compare it with other sports or hobbies.

Begin:
I think ice skating is the best (winter) sport of all. I enjoy it because … . Ice skating is much more fun than … because …

🔊 Listen

Listen to the four scenes and say what you think has just happened in each case. Some of the words below may help you.

Scene 1: bath water sing splash
Scene 2: bed light alarm clock sleep
Scene 3: drop glass vase break
Scene 4: car night splash water sink

Dictionary skills

See how fast you can find these words in your dictionary. Write down the page number for each word when you find it, and the time you took to find all six words.

president   farmer   scientist
discover   soldier   coal

Match the people with what they do.

1. a president   defends a country.
2. a farmer   cures people who are ill.
3. a scientist   rules a country.
4. a coalminer   sings to entertain people.
5. a soldier   grows and produces food.
6. a pop star   digs coal out of the ground.
7. a doctor   discovers how things work.

Game

All the people listed on the left are in a balloon which is losing height. Only one person can stay in the basket. Draw lots to decide who you are going to be and persuade the rest of the group why you should stay in the basket.

A soldier is much more important than a pop star because…

Grammar Lessons 6-10

Present perfect with yet, just *and* already

Have you	started	your	job?
Has he		his	

I haven't	started it yet.
He hasn't	

I've	just	found a job.
He's	already	gone to Europe.
She's		

Imperative for directions

Take the	train	to Maidstone.
	M20 motorway	

Get	off at	Maidstone.
Turn		

Drive down the A20 until you reach the B2163.

Turn	right	down	the B2163.
	left	along	

Turn	right	into Drayton Road.
	left	

Take the	next	turning on the	right.
	second		left.

Gerund

I	enjoy	ballooning.
	don't like	hang-gliding.

Ballooning	is	much	more fun	than	gliding.
Having a cold			worse		flying.
					feeling sick.

We were cycling along.

🔊 Dialogue

Andy and Kate have just come back from an afternoon in Dover and are very excited.

KATE: Guess who we've just seen?

MR MORGAN: Who?

ANDY: Somebody famous!

MR MORGAN: The Prime Minister?

KATE: No! Somebody much more famous than that!

MR MORGAN: The Queen?

ANDY: You're nearly right. In fact, we saw …

KATE: Princess Diana!

MR MORGAN: Really! Where? What was she doing?

KATE: She was opening an Old People's Home in Radcliffe Road.

MR MORGAN: What on earth were you doing there?

KATE: Nothing. We were cycling along when suddenly she came out of a building!

ANDY: Yes, lots of people were cheering …

KATE: So we stopped and went over to have a look …

ANDY: And then SHE came up to me and said 'Are you on holiday here?'

KATE: And do you know what? He couldn't even say a word!

1 Give short answers.

1. Did Kate and Andy see the Queen?
   No, they didn't.
2. Did they see Princess Diana?
3. Did she come out of a youth club?
4. Did the Princess speak to Andy?
5. Did Andy speak to the Princess?

Look!

We were cycling along when suddenly we saw Princess Diana.
She was opening a building when we saw her.

2 Write questions for these answers. Use the past continuous tense.

Who was visiting Dover?
Princess Diana.

1. Princess Diana.
2. An Old People's Home.
3. Cycling along.
4. Cheering.

Royal Occasions

Most of us at some time or other have seen a member of the Royal Family. We asked our readers to send us their photographs of these 'Royal Occasions' and tell us what they were doing at the time.

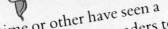

Prince Charles inspecting the wreck of the Mary Rose in Portsmouth.

Name: David McLaren
Occasion: sailing round the harbour

Princess Diana opening a youth club in Brixton.

Name: Peggy Williams
Occasion: visiting relations

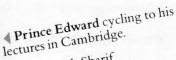

Sarah Ferguson skiing with some friends in Gstaad.

Name: Ruth Pinto
Occasion: working in a ski hotel.

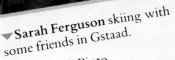

Prince Edward cycling to his lectures in Cambridge.

Name: Sadak Sharif
Occasion: working on a building site

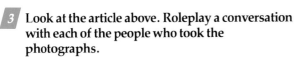

3 Look at the article above. Roleplay a conversation with each of the people who took the photographs.

YOU: Have you ever seen a member of the Royal family?
PEGGY: Yes, I have. I've seen Princess Diana.
YOU: Really? Where did you see her?
PEGGY: I saw her in Brixton when she was opening a youth club.
YOU: What were you doing there?
PEGGY: I was visiting relations.

4 Write sentences to describe each of the pictures in the article.

Peggy was visiting relations in Brixton when she saw Princess Diana.

5 Write a dialogue. You have just met somebody famous and want to tell your friend about it.

Your friend asks:
who you've just seen.
where you saw this person.
what the famous person was doing at the time.

Was I dreaming?

2 **Copy and complete these sentences as you wish.**

1. While I was having breakfast this morning, …
2. As I was coming to school, …
3. While we were watching TV, …
4. As I was walking through the park, …
5. While I was sitting on the train, …

3 **Look at the story outline below and complete the missing information.**

Context (when and where the story happened)
1. One evening last autumn I was walking in the gardens at Hampton Court.
Details (background description)
2. It was getting …
3. I was walking …
Events (what happened)
4. I saw a …
Details
5. She was …
6. She was wearing …
Events
7. I said 'The gardens …'
8. She said …
9. I looked back but …
Ending (how the story ended)
10. In a library book I found a picture of … and she was …

'One evening last autumn I was walking in the gardens at Hampton Court. It was getting dark and I was one of the last people in the gardens.

As I was walking through the rose garden I saw a young woman. She was sitting alone on a stone seat. She was crying. Her clothes were strangely old-fashioned. She was wearing a long black dress with a high collar. I went up to her and said: "Excuse me, but the gardens are closing now." She said nothing and I walked on. When I looked back at the stone seat, the woman in black was gone.

The following week, while I was looking at some history books in the library, I found a book about King Henry VIII and his six wives. In it was a picture of Anne Boleyn. She was wearing exactly the same clothes as the woman who was crying in the rose garden.'

4 📼 **Listen to Evelyn telling a frightening story.**

Note down:
  where she was working.
  what she was doing at the time.
  what she saw.

1 **Correct these statements.**

1. The writer was walking in the park.
   No, he wasn't. He was walking in the gardens at Hampton Court.
2. It was early in the morning.
3. He saw a man in the rose garden.
4. The woman was laughing.
5. She was wearing very modern clothes.
6. The woman spoke to him.

5 **Write a story about an adventure you once had. Say what happened to you.**

One day/evening last …, I was …

Did you know?

King Henry VIII's second wife, Anne Boleyn, had an extra finger on her left hand.

The Happy Prince

📟 Read and listen

Once upon a time high above a city stood the beautiful statue of the Happy Prince. His body was covered in gold and jewels. His eyes were two bright sapphires and on his sword there was a large red
5 ruby.
'The prince looks so happy!' said the citizens. 'Why can't we all be happy like him?'
   One night a swallow flew over the city. Winter was coming and he was flying south to Egypt. When he
10 saw the statue of the golden prince, he stopped to take a rest at the statue's feet. Just as he was putting his head under his wing, a large drop of water fell on him.
   The swallow looked up. He saw tears running
15 down the prince's golden cheeks.
'Who are you?' asked the swallow.
'I am the Happy Prince.'
'Then why are you crying?'
'Because of what I see,' answered the statue. 'When I
20 was alive, I never cried. I was always rich and happy. Now I am dead and from up here I can see how many people are poor and miserable. And I can only cry.'

1 In pairs, make questions from the key words and answer them.

A: Why was the statue beautiful?
B: Because it was covered in gold and jewels.

1. Why/statue/beautiful?
2. Where/ruby?
3. Where/swallow/going?
4. Why/swallow/stop?
5. Where/swallow/stop?
6. What/fall on him?
7. Why/Happy Prince/crying?

2 Copy and complete the sentences. Use each of the words in the box once only.

rain	drop	tear	water	pour	run	cry	wet

1. It was … ing with rain.
   It was pouring with rain.
2. Everything was getting …
3. Large …s of … splashed on the window.
4. There was … everywhere.
5. …s were …ing down her face.
6. I have never seen her … ing before.

3 Make a summary of the story up to 'He saw tears running down the Prince's golden cheeks'. Write only the events not the details.

Opening
Once upon a time high above a city stood the beautiful statue of the Happy Prince.
Event 1
One night a swallow flew …
Event 2
……… .
Event 3
……… .
Event 4
He looked up and saw …

Lady Jane

Read and answer.
Who was Lady Jane Grey?
How old was she when she died?
How old is the girl who plays her part?

John Ward meets the young actress Helena Bonham Carter, who plays the leading role in the film *Lady Jane*. Lady Jane Grey became Queen of England in July, 1553, at the age of sixteen. She was queen for only nine days. She was beheaded in the Tower of London in February 1554.

Helena Bonham Carter was eighteen when Trevor Nunn, director of the Royal Shakespeare Company, asked her to play the leading role in the film *Lady Jane*. At the time she was travelling round Europe with friends and hoping to go to university. The role of Lady Jane Grey sounded good and she agreed to play it.

Helena Bonham Carter is intelligent and has a good sense of humour. She is about 5'2" tall, with brown eyes, long brown hair and thick eyebrows. Trevor Nunn chose her because she looked younger than her age and could act like a child as well as an adult. I met her when she was filming on location at Dover Castle.

'I'm very self-confident,' she told me. 'At the age of thirteen I decided to be a famous actress so I went out and got an agent!'

Helena is not sure that she wants to continue making films. 'I feel confident about this film but I don't want people to think of me only as an eighteen-year-old girl who played a queen in a film and can't do anything else.'

1 Copy and complete Trevor Nunn's file on Helena.

Film: Lady Jane
Actors' File

_____

Name:

Age:

Physical description:

Part in film:

Reasons for suggesting her:

2 Roleplay the interview between John Ward and Helena Bonham Carter.

Ask Helena:
how she got the part.
how old she was.
what she was doing at the time.
when she decided to become an actress.
if she wants to continue making films.

JOHN: Helena, how did you get the part of Lady Jane Grey?
HELENA: Well, it was a surprise. Trevor Nunn asked me to play the role.
JOHN: How ...?

3 Now write their conversation.

4 Match the verbs with the correct part of the body.

1. look   mouth
2. sound   nose
3. feel   eye
4. taste   ear
5. smell   hand

Look!

It looks nice/great/good.
They look/feel fine.
That sounds exciting/wonderful.
It smells horrible/delicious.
It tastes nice/awful.

5 Respond to the remarks.

1. Come in! I'm baking some bread.
   It smells delicious!
2. We're going to have a beach barbecue tonight.
   That sounds ...
3. Do you like my new hairstyle?
4. How are the shoes? Do they feel OK?
5. What's wrong with your drink?
6. How does your new stereo sound?
7. How do you like this pudding?
8. We're going to see a film called *The Living Dead Walk Again.*

Roleplay

You are visiting the Tower of London when you see some people stealing the Crown Jewels. Use the pictures to roleplay a conversation with a police officer.

The police officer wants to know:
who you are.
what you saw.
what the robbers were wearing.
what they were carrying.
if there were any other people with them.

Now write the dialogue.

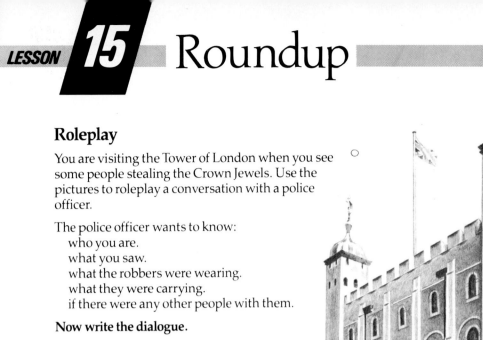

📼 Listen

Listen to Jane talking about a famous person she once saw. Copy the chart and complete the information.

Time of year: Name of famous person: Place: Event:

Writing

Complete the story by filling in the details.

It was early one autumn evening when I decided to go for a walk through the forest before going to bed.
Describe the forest
I pulled the jacket tightly round me.
Describe the weather
Suddenly I heard a noise. I looked up, frightened. And then I laughed.
Describe what you saw

Dictionary skills

A dictionary uses abbreviations for parts of speech (grammar words), for example:

　　v = verb　　*n* = noun　　*adj* = adjective

Sort these words into groups of verbs, nouns and adjectives. Then put the words in each group into alphabetical order.

sword *n*	sapphire *n*	poor *adj*	crowd *n*
cry *v*	miserable *adj*	fall *v*	crown *n*
happy *adj*	cheer *v*	rich *adj*	steal *v*
cycle *v*	family *n*	sad *adj*	seat *n*

▦ Grammar Lessons 11-15

Past continuous

	were you		doing?
What	was	he she	

We were cycling along.

He She	was	working on a building site. opening a building.

Past continuous contrasted with past simple

She was visiting relatives	when	she	saw Princess Diana.
They were cycling along		they	

Time clauses with as and while

As While	I was walking through the rose garden, I saw a young woman.

Stative verbs (which do not take the present continuous)

It That	looks feels sounds smells tastes	nice. exciting. delicious. awful.

You're from AIP, aren't you?

WINDSOR SAFARI PARK

More to see...More to do

- Killer Whale, Dolphin and Sea Lion Shows
- Birds of Prey Show* • Parrot Show
- Daily feeding of the Big Cats
- Hundreds of Wild Animals in drive through reserves • Licensed Bars and Cafeterias • Free on park transport • All inclusive admission

*Summer only

OPEN EVERY DAY FROM 10am

REGULAR GREEN LINE SERVICES

Throughout the summer Green Line 702 provides a daily, fast and direct link from Central London to the Safari Park.
All inclusive travel and admission ticket – for details telephone 01-668 7261. **GREEN LINE ⟩⟩**

TO BRITAIN'S MOST EXCITING DAY OUT

Read the advertisement and answer the questions.

1. What is the name of the Safari Park?
2. What bird shows can you see?
3. How often do they feed the Big Cats?
4. How often is the park open?
5. What time does it open?
6. Do people usually walk through the park?
7. Which is the best bus to take to the park?

📼 Dialogue

RICK:	Hello, Mr Wright. I've come to help for the day.
MR WRIGHT:	Ah, yes. You're from AIP, aren't you?
RICK:	That's right. I've brought a friend with me – Andy. That's OK, isn't it?
MR WRIGHT:	Sure. Hi, Andy.
ANDY:	Hi.
MR WRIGHT:	Have you been to the Safari Park before?
ANDY:	Yes, twice.
RICK:	I haven't. I've never really liked zoos. It seems cruel to keep animals in captivity.
MR WRIGHT:	Right, but here the animals are free to roam.
RICK:	Mmm. Sort of …
MR WRIGHT:	Come on, Andy. I bet you've never fed a killer whale!

1 Which is correct?

1. a) Rick is just visiting the Safari Park.
   b) Rick is going to do some work at the Safari Park.

2. a) He has often been to the park.
   b) This is his first visit to the park.

3. a) He thinks zoos are cruel.
   b) He doesn't like animals very much.

2 **Copy and complete these sentences with a question tag.**

1. It's beautiful, …?
2. She's from Dover, …?
3. You aren't coming tomorrow, …?
4. He was ill, …?
5. Your mother doesn't like roses, …?
6. They enjoy school, …?
7. She hasn't finished yet, …?
8. I've seen you somewhere before, …?

3 **Write down four things you know about your partner. Check the facts by using question tags.**

Write:
  his or her age.
  his or her taste in food/drink/music.
  where he or she buys clothes.
  where he or she has been on holiday.

A: You're fourteen, aren't you?
B: Yes, I am.
A: You aren't English, are you?
B: No, I'm not.

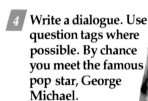

4 **Write a dialogue. Use question tags where possible. By chance you meet the famous pop star, George Michael.**

Make sure it is him.
Ask him to sign your autograph book.
You have heard he is doing a concert in your town next week. Check this and thank him.
Say goodbye.

Six days a week

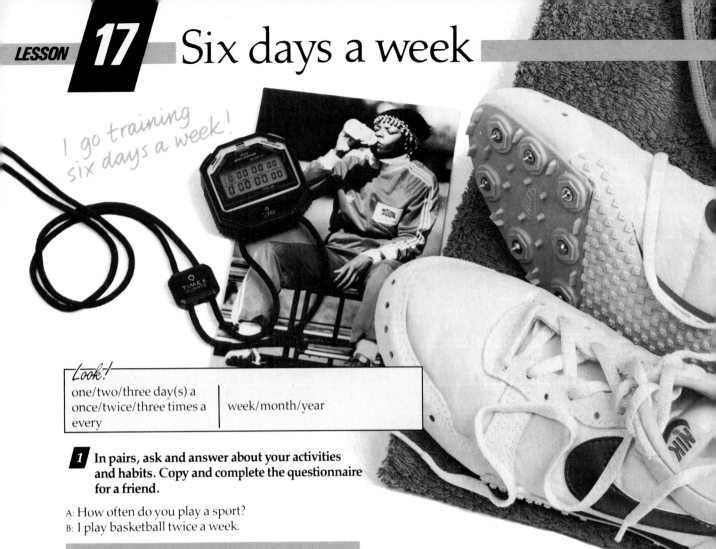

I go training six days a week!

Look!

one/two/three day(s) a once/twice/three times a every	week/month/year

1 In pairs, ask and answer about your activities and habits. Copy and complete the questionnaire for a friend.

A: How often do you play a sport?
B: I play basketball twice a week.

A profile of you and your habits

Sporting and leisure activities

How often do you: play a sport?
go swimming/running/training?
go to the cinema?
watch TV?
What else do you do in your spare time?
How much time do you spend on it?

Family activities

How often do you: visit your grandparents?
go to a restaurant with your parents?
go to church?
help in the house?
get the lunch ready?

Health and hygiene

How often do you: go to the dentist?
clean your teeth?
stay up after midnight?
wash your hair?

2 Choose one section from the questionnaire. Write about your partner's activities.

Rebecca goes to gym classes twice a week. She also goes swimming for an hour every Sunday morning. She likes films and goes to the cinema twice a month. She doesn't spend much time watching TV. On average she watches TV one or two evenings a week. She also likes reading in her spare time.

3 Now choose a section from the questionnaire and write about your activities or habits.

Did you know?
Humans blink approximately twenty-five times a minute.

FRANCES JEATER
ce cream man .CHRIS SANDERS
Colin ....IAN MERCER
Co-pilot.............EDMUND PEGGE
Produced by BILL SELLARS
Directed by RICHARD BRAMALL *(R)*
★ CEEFAX SUBTITLES

TUESDAY
BBC 1

NEW SERIES
10.0 Miami Vice

The return of the Emmy Award-winning series starring **Don Johnson** as Sonny Crockett and **Philip Michael Thomas** as Ricardo Tubbs also starring **Phil Collins** as Phil Mayhew *Phil the Shill* Conning innocent dupes like Switek in a bogus game show comes easily for a charming

for him without striking back with a vengeance. Singer-songwriter Phil Collins makes his television acting début as slick con artist Phil. Lt Castillo
　　　EDWARD JAMES OLMOS
Switek..........MICHAEL TALBOTT
Zito ....JOHN DIEHL
Gina...........SAUNDRA SANTIAGO
Trudy ....OLIVIA BROWN
Izzy Moreno ..MARTIN FERRERO

Approximately 95 per cent of homes in Britain have a TV. There are four colour channels: BBC 1, BBC 2, ITV and Channel 4. Programmes start at 6.30 in the morning and continue until after midnight. The channels broadcast a total of 50 hours of programmes a day, seven days a week. According to a recent survey, people watch between three and four hours a day. It seems most teenagers would rather watch crime series like 'Miami Vice' and quiz programmes like 'Mastermind' than the news or documentaries.

1 **Answer.**

1. How many TV channels are there in Britain?
2. How many days a week do they broadcast?
3. How many hours a day, on average, do people watch TV in Britain?

2 In pairs, ask and answer the same questions about TV in your country.

3 Write a paragraph about TV in your country. Use the text to help you.

There are … TV channels …

Look!
I quite like
I enjoy
I don't like　(watching) sports programmes.
I prefer
I'd rather watch comedies than documentaries.

4 Write down three TV programmes you enjoy watching and say what kind they are. Talk to your partner about them.

Choose from:
comedy programmes
crime series
documentaries
films
nature programmes
the news

plays
quiz programmes
soap operas
sports events
variety shows

A: Do you like comedy programmes?
B: Yes, I like 'Taxi'.
A: Yes, I quite like 'Taxi' but I'd rather watch 'Miami Vice'.

5 In groups, compare your favourite programmes and find out which are the three most popular.

6 Listen to Chloe and Nicky talking about watching television. Copy and complete the chart.

	Chloe	Nicky
How much TV they watch		
Programmes they like		
Programmes they don't like (if any)		

Dolphins in captivity

Read and answer.
How long do dolphins live in captivity?
Why are dolphins popular entertainers?
Is a killer whale dangerous?

Dolphins and killer whales, which are the largest members of the dolphin species, have recently become popular entertainers. They are friendly and intelligent. They seem to have a great sense of fun and they are able to perform wonderful tricks.

Winnie, a killer whale in Windsor Safari Park, performs three times a day. She does a series of tricks. For example, she climbs out of her pool, blows a trumpet and swims round with a pair of sunglasses on her head. 'Of course it is commercial,' says her trainer. 'But they enjoy performing tricks.' However, a number of scientists believe that keeping dolphins and killer whales in captivity shortens their lives and that performing the same tricks every day is not good for them.

Since 1969 at least fifty-seven dolphins and nine killer whales have come to Britain. Of these, only seventeen dolphins and four killer whales are still alive. Dolphins in the wild usually live for more than thirty years. In captivity, however, most die before their twelfth birthday. Killer whales can live for as long as thirty-five years but in Britain they live on average no more than two or three years.

A Swiss professor says: 'Basically you are always going to get problems when you keep animals in small spaces when they are used to being free.'

Once people called them 'killers of the seas', but this is a myth. Although killer whales eat many forms of sea-life, they are not dangerous to man.

Look!

Dolphins in the wild usually live for more than thirty years.
In captivity, however, most die before their twelfth birthday.
However, in captivity most die before their twelfth birthday.

1 **Match the sentences in the two lists below and join them using** however.

1. Killer whales can live for many years in the wild.
2. Killer whales are called 'killers of the sea'.
3. Many people think dolphins enjoy performing tricks.
4. Many people think whales are fish.

a) Like the seal and dolphin, they are mammals.
b) Scientific tests show it is not healthy for them.
c) In captivity, most die young.
d) They very rarely attack human beings.

Look!

Although dolphins in the wild usually live for more than thirty years, in captivity most die young.

2 **Now rewrite the sentences in exercise 1 starting with** although.

Although killer whales …, in captivity …

3 **Write an article about killer whales for your school magazine. First make notes.**

Name: Killer whale
Species:
Natural habitat: The sea
Normal lifespan:
Average lifespan in captivity:
Reasons for being popular performers:
Examples of what they can do:

Begin:
Killer whales are members of the dolphin species.
They usually live … and in the wild they …

Did you know?
A blue whale can survive for six months without eating. It lives on its own fat.

Cristina Bianco
Sabina Conti ?

Roleplay

You are interviewing a new TV star called Sabina.
Check your information about her, using question
tags.

A: Hello, Sabina. You're Italian, aren't you?
B: Yes, that's right.
A: And you can ...

CONTI S.M.

Full name:	CONTI Sabina Marie
Nationality:	Italian
Languages:	Speaks Italian, French and English fluently.
Parents:	Mother Swiss. Father Italian. Both work for Italian TV.
Home town:	Turin
Acting experience:	Played leading part in the TV series 'Texas'.

BTV

 Listen

Listen to this interview with a TV actor.
Make notes about:
   how long he has worked in TV.
   if he likes it.
   what sort of parts he's played.
   what he's acting in now.
   how he likes to relax.

Write

Imagine you are the actor. Use your notes from the
listening exercise to write a paragraph about your
work and how you like to relax.

Game

One person is in the 'hot seat'. The rest of you must ask this person questions. He or she must answer them without saying yes or no. See how long you can last in the 'hot seat'!

A: Your name's Robert, isn't it?
B: My name isn't Robert. It's John.

Dictionary skills

Sort these words into parts of speech. Then copy and complete the sentences.

fast *adv*   hers *pron*   in *prep*   well *adv*
but *conj*   it *pron*   under *prep*   and *conj*
quickly *adv*   to *prep*   so *conj*   she *pron*

1. He likes fish … he doesn't like chips. *(conj)*
2. He can write English very … . *(adv)*
3. … trains dolphins. *(pron)*
4. Put your bag … your seat. *(prep)*

Grammar Lessons 16-20

Question tags

You're English,	aren't	you?		You	aren't	English, going now,	are	you?
They're going now,		they?		They				they?

It was expensive, wasn't it?		It wasn't expensive, was it?
He lives here, doesn't he?		He doesn't live here, does he?
You've been here before, haven't you?		You haven't been here before, have you?

Adverbial phrases of time

How often do you play basketball?

I play basketball	two hours three days once twice three times	a	day. week. month. year.

Modal would rather

I would They would	rather watch	'Miami Vice' comedies	than	'Dynasty'. documentaries.

Adverb of contrast however

Dolphins in the wild usually live for more than 30 years.

However, in captivity In captivity, however,	most die before their twelfth birthday.

Clause of concession

Although dolphins in the wild usually live for more than 30 years, in captivity most die young.

It may hurt a little.

📼 Dialogue

DENTIST:	Open wide. How's school?
KATE:	Errgh!
DENTIST:	Good. You only need one small filling. I'll do it now. OK?
KATE:	Urrgh!
DENTIST:	I'll have to use the drill, I'm afraid. Do you want an injection?
KATE:	Will it hurt?
DENTIST:	It may hurt a little but only for a few seconds.
KATE:	All right.
DENTIST:	There! That didn't hurt much, did it? Now you won't feel the drill at all.
KATE:	Arrgh!

Look!
Degrees of possibility:

It will hurt.	It's definitely going to hurt.
It may hurt.	It's possibly going to hurt.
It won't hurt.	It's definitely not going to hurt.

---

1 True or False?

1. Kate is at the doctor's.
2. She needs a filling.
3. The dentist says he'll fill her tooth tomorrow.
4. The dentist will have to use the drill.
5. The injection won't hurt at all.

YOUR KITCHEN MAY NOT BE AS SAFE AS YOU THINK!

BE SURE, BE SAFE, BE CAREFUL IN THE HOME!

2 Comment on the picture. Use may **with the words in the box to say what may happen to the little boy.**

burn/cut/hurt himself on the ...
knock over the ...
break the ...
fall off/over/out of the ...

3 In pairs or groups, talk about two of the following topics. Use may, will **or** won't **in your discussion.**

1. The success of your country's athletes in the next Olympics.
2. The future successes of your favourite football team.
3. The future success of a rock band or rock star.
4. The lives of the characters in a current TV series.

A: Do you think we will win any medals in the next Olympics?
B: We may win a silver or bronze in the athletics. But we won't win a gold!

4 Write a dialogue. You are at the dentist's. The dentist looks at your teeth.

The dentist says he needs to take out a tooth.
You want to know if it will hurt or not.
The dentist says it won't hurt with an injection but it may hurt a little afterwards.

Joke time!
PATIENT: Doctor! Doctor! I don't know what's the matter with me. Half the time I don't know where I am.
DENTIST: Open wide!

Boys used to wear caps.

People leaving for →
Dover in a horse-drawn
coach.

Slum children eating
eel-and-meat pies
costing twopence each. ↘

↑ Swimmers enjoying a
day at the seaside.

Young children
working in a
brickyard in 1871.

Look!

Boys used to wear caps on their heads.
Poor children didn't use to wear shoes.

1 **Look at the pictures and describe what life used to be like in the nineteenth and early twentieth centuries.**

Describe:
    what poor children used to wear.
    what sort of food they used to eat.
    what people used to do in summer.
    what they used to wear when they went swimming.
    how people used to travel.
    what sort of life poor children used to have.

2 **Discuss what life used to be like in the last century.**

Use the following topics:

family life	work
health	leisure
education	fashion
transport and communication	

Rich people used to have lots of servants.
Many children used to die of disease.
Poor children didn't use to go to school.

3 **Talk about how your tastes have changed. Use the words given in the box as a guide.**

food	music	leisure activities
drink	TV	friends

A: What about TV?
B: I used to watch 'Playschool'? Did you (use to watch it)?
A: Yes, I did. I used to go to my Granny's to watch it. Did you use to watch 'Ready! Steady! Go!' as well?
B: No, I didn't.

4 **Write four sentences about the changes in your tastes.**

I used to like swimming but I don't now.

5 🔲 **Listen to two people talking about their changes in taste.**

Note down the things they used to like doing when they were younger; if they still do them; what else they like doing now.

Button Button

📼 Read and listen

The parcel was lying by the front door. It was a square box, with their name and address on it in capital letters: 'MR AND MRS ARTHUR LEWIS, 217 EAST 37TH STREET, NEW YORK, NEW YORK STATE 10016.'

Norma opened it. Inside the box was a smaller box with a push button on the
5 top of it. The button was covered with glass. There was a message with it which said: 'Mr Steward will call on you at eight o'clock this evening.'

The doorbell rang at eight o'clock.

'I'll go!' Norma called from the kitchen. Arthur was in the living room, reading. There was a small man at the door. He took off his hat when he saw Norma.
10 'Mrs Lewis?' he asked, politely.

'Yes?'

'I'm Mr Steward. Can I come in?'

'I'm rather busy,' Norma answered, 'but I'll go and get your thing.'

'Don't you want to know what it is?' he said.
15 'No, I don't think so,' she replied.

'It may be valuable,' he said.

'You mean it may bring me money?'

'Money, yes'.

Norma didn't like Mr Steward very much. Then Arthur came out of the
20 living room. Mr Steward told Arthur his name. Arthur pointed towards the parcel. 'What is it actually?'

'I can explain very quickly. Can I come in?'

Arthur looked at Norma. They both hesitated. Then Arthur said: 'Well, why not?' They all went into the living room and shut the door.
25 Mr Steward sat in Norma's chair. He took a key out of his pocket and said: 'This key will open the glass cover on the button-machine.' He put the key on a coffee table by his chair. 'The bell,' he said, 'is connected to our office.'

'What is it for?' asked Arthur.

'If you press the button,' Mr Steward told him, 'someone will die somewhere in
30 the world – someone you don't know. If you do this, I'll pay you fifty thousand dollars.'

---

1 Write the sentences in the correct order to make a summary of the text.

1. On the small box was a message saying that a man called Mr Steward was going to call at eight o'clock.
2. Inside the parcel was a small box with a button on it.
3. He told them they could earn $50,000 by pressing the button.
4. One day Norma and Arthur Lewis found a parcel outside their front door.
5. He said he wanted to explain about the box.
6. At eight o'clock that evening Mr Steward rang their doorbell.
7. It had their name and address on it.
8. In the end Norma and Arthur invited Mr Steward into the livingroom.

One day Norma and Arthur Lewis found a parcel outside their front door.

2 Complete the passage. Use each of the verbs of speaking in the box once only.

said called answered explained asked

The doorbell rang.
'I'll go!' ... the girl to her mother upstairs.
She opened the door. There was a man with a tool box.
'Yes, what do you want?' she ... .
'I'm from the telephone company,' he ... .
The girl looked puzzled.
'I've come to check your telephone,' he ... .
'Oh, fine,' she ... politely. 'Do come in.'

Nice teeth, nice smile!

Read and answer.
How much sugar does one adult eat in a week?
Are children's teeth better today than they used to be?
Are apples really good for cleaning your teeth?

What makes a nice smile? Most dentists would say
'Nice teeth', but how many people can boast a healthy
set of teeth nowadays?
You may not believe it but most of the food we eat
today is bad for our teeth. A hundred years ago we
used to eat on average a kilo of sugar each year. Now
we eat a kilo of sugar a week. So, what do dentists say
we should eat and drink if we want to look after our
teeth? Surprisingly, it seems that cheese, peanuts,
crisps and bread are all right. Not so good, however,
are ice-lollies, icecream, chocolate, chewing-gum and
apples. (Yes, apples! The acid causes tooth decay.) But
the real tooth-rotters are biscuits, sweet fizzy drinks,
toffees and boiled sweets.

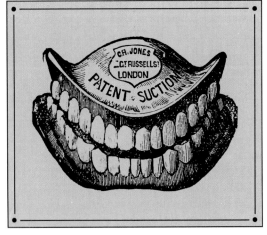

*An advertisement from 1880 for a
pair of false teeth.*

1 Make a list of all the food and drink in the text
above. Do a survey of the people in your group.
Find out how often they eat or drink the items
mentioned. Complete a chart like the one below.

Food	John	Sue
cheese	every day	never
peanuts	once a week	twice a week
crisps	often	hardly ever
bread	every day	every day

2 **Now write a report. Use the results of your survey.**

Most people eat/drink...every day. Not many people...

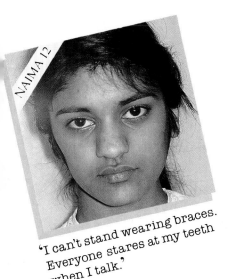

'I can't stand wearing braces. Everyone stares at my teeth when I talk.'

'I used to hate going to the dentist but I don't mind it now. Last time I didn't need any fillings and Mum gave me five pounds.'

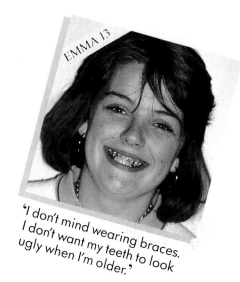

'I don't mind wearing braces. I don't want my teeth to look ugly when I'm older.'

'I can't stand going to the dentist. I hate the sound of the drill and the smell.'

'I'm frightened of going to the dentist. It always hurts. And I hate the taste of metal in my mouth.'

Look!

I can't stand going to the dentist.
I don't mind wearing braces.

---

3 **True or False?**

1. Naima hates wearing braces.
2. Louise doesn't mind going to the dentist.
3. Harry is frightened of going to the dentist.
4. Steve had five fillings last time he went.
5. Emma wears braces.

4 **Find out if your partner likes or dislikes the same things as you.**

A: I can't stand going to the dentist.
B: No, nor can I./Oh, I don't mind it.
A: I like going shopping with my mother.
B: Yes, so do I./Oh, I can't stand it.

Ask about:
  going to the dentist.
  going shopping with your mother.
  buying new clothes.
  doing the washing up.
  staying at home on Saturday night.
  going to visit your relations.
  dressing up for special occasions.

Look at the pictures and read the conversation.

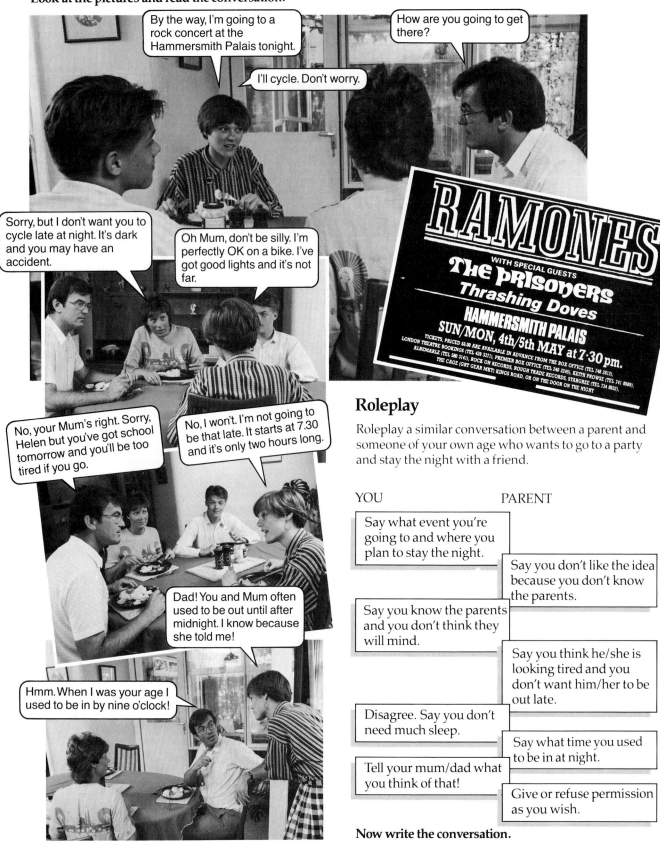

Roleplay

Roleplay a similar conversation between a parent and someone of your own age who wants to go to a party and stay the night with a friend.

YOU	PARENT
Say what event you're going to and where you plan to stay the night.	
	Say you don't like the idea because you don't know the parents.
Say you know the parents and you don't think they will mind.	
	Say you think he/she is looking tired and you don't want him/her to be out late.
Disagree. Say you don't need much sleep.	
	Say what time you used to be in at night.
Tell your mum/dad what you think of that!	
	Give or refuse permission as you wish.

Now write the conversation.

🔊 Listen

Listen to this person talking about his childhood.
Copy and complete the information in the box.

> Where he grew up:
> How he went to school:
> What he used to do in the evenings:
> Where he used to go for his holiday:

Write

How much do you know about your parents'
childhood? Find out what life used to be like for them.

Write sentences about:
   the sort of hairstyles and clothes they used to wear.
   what they used to watch on television.
   how much pocket money they used to get.
   how old they were when they went out with girls
   or boys.

Dictionary skills

In each of these words there is a spelling mistake. Find
the words in your dictionary and correct the spelling.

1. seperate *adj*   4. sucessful *adj*   7. marrage *n*
2. incredable *adj*   5. emmigrate *v*   8. recieve *v*
3. beautifull *adj*   6. rythm *n*   9. knifes *n (plural)*

Joke time!

MAN: I don't know what's the matter with me.
        I keep seeing into the future.
WOMAN: When did this start?
MAN: Next Tuesday!

▪ Grammar Lessons 21-25

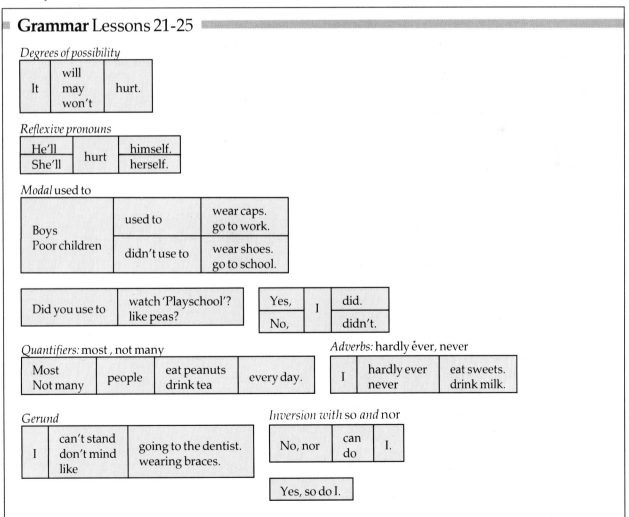

Degrees of possibility

It	will may won't	hurt.

Reflexive pronouns

He'll She'll	hurt	himself. herself.

Modal used to

Boys Poor children	used to	wear caps. go to work.
	didn't use to	wear shoes. go to school.

Did you use to	watch 'Playschool'? like peas?		Yes, No,	I	did. didn't.

Quantifiers: most, not many

Most Not many	people	eat peanuts drink tea	every day.

Adverbs: hardly ever, never

I	hardly ever never	eat sweets. drink milk.

Gerund

I	can't stand don't mind like	going to the dentist. wearing braces.

Inversion with so *and* nor

No, nor	can do	I.

Yes, so do I.

If I hit the spaceship...

🔊 **Dialogue**

ANDY: Eight thousand! That's my best score
         so far.
TOM: Come on, Andy. We'd better go. If we miss
         the last bus, my dad'll be angry with me.
ANDY: Hang on. Just one more game. If I hit the
         spaceship, I'll stop.
TOM: OK. Have you got 20p?
ANDY: No, only a pound. I'll go and change it.
BOY 1:   *(twisting Andy's arm and taking the money)*
         I'll have that.
ANDY: Give me back my money!
BOY 2:   Shut up! It's ours now.
TOM: I'll call the manager if you don't give it
         back.
BOY 1:   If you do that, you'll be in big trouble!
MANAGER: Now then. What's going on here?
         Go on home, you lot.
         You're nothing but
         trouble.
BOY 2:   Come on, Rocky, leave
         'em alone. Let's get
         out of here.

Look!

If I hit the spaceship, I'll stop.
If you don't give my money back, I'll call the
manager.

---

1 **Complete these sentences from the dialogue.**

1. If we … the bus, my dad'll …
2. If I … the spaceship, … stop.
3. If you … give it back, … the manager.
4. If you call the manager, …

41

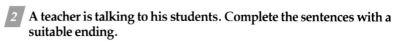

2 A teacher is talking to his students. Complete the sentences with a suitable ending.

If you don't do your homework, you'll fail your exams.

1. If you don't do your homework,	I'll let you go home early.
2. If you're rude to me again,	I'll give you a holiday.
3. If you don't work harder,	you'll fail your exams.
4. If you finish this exercise quickly,	you'll enjoy your holiday in England.
5. If you do well in your exams,	I'll stop the school trip.
6. If you learn to speak English,	I'll write to your parents.

3 Write captions for the pictures starting with if he/she …, he/she'll … .

1. run/catch/bus

2. go now/be late/school

3. fall/break

4. eat/be ill

4 Write a dialogue. Your friend's five-year-old brother has taken your diary.

You ask him to give it back but he refuses.
You offer to give him some sweets but he still refuses.
You offer to buy him an icecream as well.
He accepts and gives it back.

Begin like this:

YOU: Give me back my diary, please!
BOY: No, I won't!
YOU: If …

Did you know?
There are over 4,000 man-made objects flying in outer space.

If you don't find them...

Starcrash!

You are the captain of a spaceship which has crashed on a strange planet. There are dangerous, flesh-eating creatures everywhere. You have captured an enemy spaceship and you want to take off and escape as quickly as possible. However, to be able to fight the creatures and escape you must find a sword, a laser gun and the instruction manual to fly the enemy spaceship. If you don't find all three, you won't be able to leave the planet.

HOW TO PLAY THE GAME

Put the numbers 1-9 in a hat. Person A takes out all the numbers one at a time and reads them out. There is an instruction for each number. Person B must tell person A what will happen if she/he follows the instruction.

A: My first number is eight. What will happen if I shoot the creatures?
B: If you shoot the creatures, they'll kill you.
A: My second number is . . . What will happen if I . . .

How many numbers did you read before you found the sword, the laser gun and the manual? Now play the game again with A and B reversing roles.

KEY TO THE NUMBERS

Instruction	What will happen
1. Look behind the satellite door.	9. The ship will explode.
2. Signal S.O.S.	7. You'll float in space.
3. Open the digital desk.	2. The creatures will hear you.
4. Step out of the spaceship.	6. You'll never wake up.
5. Look under the computer.	3. You'll find the laser gun.
6. Go to sleep.	8. They'll kill you.
7. Try to run.	1. You'll find the sword.
8. Shoot the creatures.	4. The creatures will see you.
9. Take off without the manual.	5. You'll find the manual.

1 Answer.

1. What is your job?
2. Why are you on a strange planet?
3. What are you going to escape in?
4. Why is the situation dangerous?
5. What do you need to be able to escape?

2 In pairs, play the Starcrash game.

Look!
If you don't find all three things, you won't be able to take off.

3 Complete these sentences from the game.

1. If you don't look behind the satellite door, you won't find ...
2. If you don't ... the digital desk, you ...
3. If you don't ... the computer, ...

4 Copy and complete these sentences.

1. If you don't put stamps on letters, they won't ...
2. If you don't write clearly, the teacher won't ...
3. If you don't leave now, ...
4. If you don't wear braces on your teeth, ...
5. If you don't go to school, ...

Joke time!

One bird said to another, 'Look there's a space rocket. I wish I could fly like that.'
The other bird said, 'You could, if your bottom was on fire!'

You must run faster.

📼 Read and listen

Kirsty wins through!

1. This time, Kirsty, you must run faster.

2.

3. Sorry, Kirsty. You're not fit enough. You must train more regularly and you must train much harder!

4. And so Kirsty trains hard every day…and night!.

Three weeks later…

5.

6.

7. Gail was right! Regular training makes you a superstar!

If you run as fast as this tomorrow, you'll win a medal for the club!

Look!

You must	run faster.
	train harder.
	train more regularly.

---

1 Match the sentences with the correct pictures.

1. Kirsty decides to train hard.
2. Gail is pleased with her and praises her.
3. Kirsty loses the race.
4. Kirsty wins a gold medal.
5. Gail is annoyed with Kirsty and criticises her.
6. Gail tells Kirsty that she must run faster in the race.

2 Use the sentences from exercise 1 to write a summary about what happened to Kirsty.

3 📼 Listen to a runner talking about his training.

Note down:
> how often he trains.
> how his training schedule has changed.
> the differences between winter and summer training.

4 Complete the sentences with one of the verbs and adjectives below. Change the adjectives into comparative adverbs each time.

work/hard	save/regular	go to bed/early
eat/sensible	run/fast	behave/good

1. If you …, you won't get in the school team.
   If you don't run faster, you won't get into the school team.
2. If you …, you'll get tooth decay.
3. If you …, you won't pass your exams.
4. If you …, you'll feel tired all day.
5. If you …, you'll have to stay in.
6. If you …, you'll never be able to buy the radio.

5 Write a paragraph for a magazine for young people about careers in sport.

Say what you have to do to be a runner (using your notes from the listening exercise) or choose another sport.

Read and answer.
How do stars begin?
Why do they shine?
What is the Milky Way?

If you look up into the sky on a clear night, you will see millions of stars. If you look more closely, you will see how some stars make patterns and pictures. These are called constellations. A constellation which is easy to find is The Plough (Ursa Minor).

Many constellations are used as the signs of the zodiac. The word 'zodiac' comes from an old Greek word for 'animals' because many of the constellations look like animals.

Every star begins its life as a very thin cloud of hydrogen gas. As the cloud gets smaller, all the atoms of gas in the centre get very hot until finally the cloud begins to shine as a star. In fact, you don't see the star itself, you see the light that shines from it.

All stars are different colours and some of them shine more brightly than others. The colour of each star depends on its temperature. Some stars have a temperature of 1,500°C. Other stars can be as hot as 100,000°C. The hottest stars are white.

Not all stars live for the same length of time. The life of a star can vary from a few million years to 10,000 million years. The small, dim stars live much longer than the very hot, bright ones. These burn out much faster.

A galaxy is a collection of millions of stars. The Earth, the Sun and the planets are all part of the Milky Way galaxy. Astronomers believe that there are 100,000 million stars in the Milky Way.

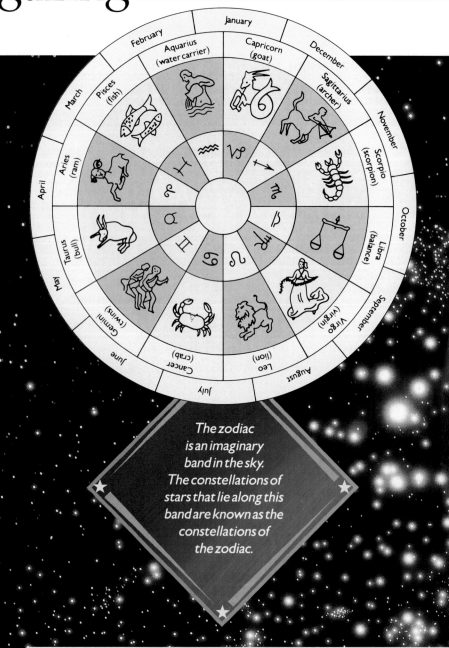

The zodiac is an imaginary band in the sky. The constellations of stars that lie along this band are known as the constellations of the zodiac.

The colours of stars

Although stars look white, they are not. Their colours depend on how old they are, how dense they are and how hot they are. Each star may change many times and in many different ways. Some stars are red, some are yellow and others are blue. The small ones are called dwarves, the larger ones are called giants and the largest are called supergiants. Some stars get very hot and explode. These are called supernovas.

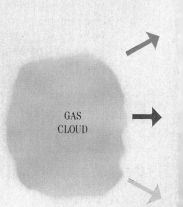

GAS CLOUD

BLUE DWARF

BLUE GIANT

RED DWARF

RED GIANT

RED SUPERGIANT

SUPERNOVA

YELLOW DWARF

YELLOW GIANT

YELLOW SUPERGIANT

1 Which is correct?

1. The Plough is the name of
   a) a star.
   b) a constellation.
2. A star begins its life as a
   a) shining light.
   b) cloud of gas.
3. The colour of a star depends on
   a) how hot it is.
   b) how close it is to the Earth.
4. Bright stars
   a) live longer than dim stars.
   b) don't live as long as dim stars.

2 Write questions for these answers.

What is a constellation?
The pattern which a group of stars makes.

1. The pattern which a group of stars makes.
2. From an old Greek word meaning 'animals'.
3. It depends on their temperature.
4. White.
5. No, their ages can vary.
6. A collection of millions of stars.

Look!

All stars have different colours.
Every star has a different colour.
Many stars have a temperature of over 1,000 degrees.
Some stars are small and dim but others (other stars) are very hot and bright.

3 Complete these sentences from the text with one of the words in the box.

all	every	some	other

1. ... star begins its life as a thin cloud of gas.
2. ... stars have a temperature of 1,500 degrees Celsius.
3. Not ... stars live as long as each other.
4. Some stars shine more brightly than ... stars.

4 In groups, discuss if the following generalisations are true or false.

1. All birds can fly.
2. All fish live in the water.
3. All reptiles lay eggs.
4. All trees lose their leaves in winter.
5. All rivers flow into the sea.
6. All plants need soil.

Palmistry—the art of palm reading

Palm reading, or palmistry, is many thousands of years old and has developed into a science. It can tell us a lot about someone's personality and talents but it will not necessarily tell us what will happen to them in the future. A professional palmist first looks at the whole hand and studies its shape and texture. Next the palmist studies the fingers, and finally the lines of the hand.

Clear hand lines   Main hand lines which are clear and strong indicate someone who is even-tempered and happy with life. This sort of person will not get angry quickly and will be very careful about getting involved in anything. At work, they will be quiet, careful and methodical.

Small hand lines   A hand which has a lot of small lines indicates someone who is sensitive and gets angry quickly and suddenly. People like this are nervous and often get excited. They will usually be talented and will probably have a number of different hobbies.

The Heart Line   If you have a strong Heart Line, you are warm and loving. If you have a weak line, you are quite a cool person. If you have a lot of little lines coming off the Heart Line, you will have a lot of romance in your life.

The Head Line   If you have a strong Head Line, you are very intelligent and you will get a good job.

The Life Line   If you have a long Life Line, you will live a long time.

The Saturn Line   If the Saturn Line is clear and goes as far as the middle finger, you will be successful.

The Heart Line

The Head Line

The Life Line

The Saturn Line

Answer
1. What can palmistry tell you about a person?
2. What are the three main stages in palm reading? (First, the palmist …)
3. Will a cool, calm person probably have strong clear lines or many small lines on their hand?
4. Which lines in your palm tell you about:
    your personality?
    how long you will live?
    how successful you will be?
    how intelligent you are?

Word study

List all the adjectives from the text and make two columns. In one column write all the adjectives which you think apply to you and in the other those which do not.

Use the information in the text to read each other's palms. Do you agree with the analysis?

 Listen

Listen to Ben talking on 'Problem Phone-in'. Answer True or False.

1. He has no job.
2. He doesn't like his job.
3. The job he's got has no future.
4. He wants to go to college.
5. His mother is not able to work.
6. His mother doesn't want him to go to college.

Write

Write Ben's letter to a magazine asking for advice. Say what the problem is and what choices are possible.

Begin and end your letter like this:

> Ben's address
> Date

Dear Helpline,
 My problem is this: I ...

What do you think I should do?
 Yours sincerely,
 Ben Turner

Dictionary skills

Look up the word *palmistry* in your dictionary. Find the part which tells you:
 what part of speech it is.
 how to pronounce it.
 what it means.
Write down the word for *palmistry* in your own language.

Grammar Lessons 26-30

First conditional (if clauses)

If I	hit the spaceship,	I'll stop.
	miss the bus,	he'll be angry.

I'll stop	if I	hit the spaceship.
He'll be angry		miss the bus.

What will happen if I shoot the creatures?

If you don't give me my money back, I'll call the manager. I'll call the manager if you don't give me my money back.

If you don't look under the computer, you won't find the manual. You won't find the manual if you don't look under the computer.

Comparison of adverbs

You must	run work train	faster. harder. more regularly.

The dim stars live much longer than the bright ones.

Quantifiers

All		have different colours.
Some	stars	are brighter than others.
Many		have a temperature of over 1,000°C.
Every star has a different colour.		

I've got to go on a course.

🖾 Dialogue

GRANNY: Are you going to Auntie Megan's party next week?

ANDY: No, I'm afraid we can't. I've got to go to Birmingham with the chess team.

KATE: And I've got to go on a survival course with the school.

GRANNY: That sounds fun.

KATE: It won't be!

ANDY: They've got to learn how to look after themselves out of doors.

KATE: We've got to build ourselves a shelter, put up a tent, make a fire …

ANDY: And they've got to cook their own food. It'll taste horrible, I bet!

KATE: It won't!

GRANNY: Well, I hope you enjoy yourselves.

KATE: Don't worry, Gran. We will!

1 **Copy and complete the notice for the school noticeboard.**

The Youth Survival Course teaches young people how to … . The course includes training in the following skills:
How to:
   1. build a …
   2. …
   3. …
   4. …
Please contact Penny Gardener for more details.

> *Look!*
> I've got to go to Birmingham.

2 **In pairs, choose an event and an excuse and make conversations like this:**

A: Are you coming to the disco?
B: No, I'm afraid I can't.
A: Why not?
B: I've got to visit my grandmother.

EVENTS	EXCUSES
disco	do my homework
party at Andy's	go to the dentist
barbecue at the youth club	visit my grandmother
	babysit for my brother
cinema	go to my violin class
swimming gala	

3 📼 **Listen to these parents telephoning the school secretary. Copy and complete the information.**

> Name of pupil:
> Class:
> Cannot attend:
> Reason:

4 **Write a note from one of the parents confirming the telephone conversation.**

Begin:

Dear Mrs Shepherd,
        This is just to confirm that Billy cannot …
because …

> *Look!*
>
> *Reflexives*
>
> | myself | ourselves |
> |---|---|
> | yourself | yourselves |
> | himself | themselves |
> | herself | |
> | itself | |

5 **In pairs, complete the questionnaire.**

A: What do you do to amuse yourself when it rains?
B: I sometimes play 'Patience'.
A: Do you? I usually read.

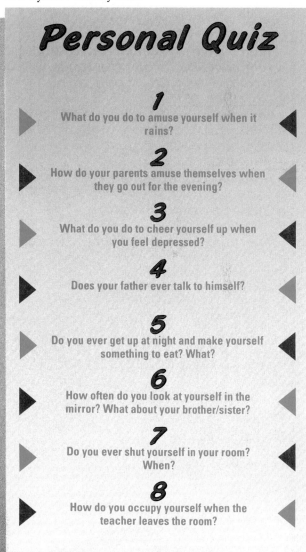

Personal Quiz

1 What do you do to amuse yourself when it rains?

2 How do your parents amuse themselves when they go out for the evening?

3 What do you do to cheer yourself up when you feel depressed?

4 Does your father ever talk to himself?

5 Do you ever get up at night and make yourself something to eat? What?

6 How often do you look at yourself in the mirror? What about your brother/sister?

7 Do you ever shut yourself in your room? When?

8 How do you occupy yourself when the teacher leaves the room?

Joke time!

JACK: Are you coming to the school disco?
JILL: No, I've got to help my father with my homework.

Ever since November…

Last November, Des was trying to row single-handed across the Pacific Ocean when there was a storm. He was shipwrecked on a desert island and has been living there ever since. It is now the middle of December and a rescue ship has just arrived at the island. The captain wants to find out how Des has managed to survive on the desert island for so long. Fortunately, Des kept a diary.

> **NOVEMBER 15TH**
> Not a bad island. Plenty of coconuts and bananas so I won't die of hunger or thirst. I cut down some palm leaves and made myself a small shelter.
> **NOVEMBER 19TH**
> Made myself a fishing rod today. Caught some fish from the lagoon. Delicious! No sign of any ship.
> **NOVEMBER 25TH**
> Amused myself today – made a bamboo pipe and am now learning how to play it.
> **NOVEMBER 30TH**
> Went to the other side of the island. Found three more shells for my collection.
> **DECEMBER 6TH**
> I've been living on this island for three weeks! When will somebody come?

> **Look!**
> How long have you been living here?
> I've been living here since November.
> He's been living there for three weeks.

1 In pairs, roleplay the conversation between the captain and Des. Use Des's diary for the answers.

The captain asks:
   how long Des has been living there.
   where he has been sleeping.
   what he has been eating and drinking.
   how he has been amusing himself.

2 Write the conversation.

3 In pairs, think of things you know about your teacher and your partner. Ask them how long they have been doing these things.

How long have you been living in … ?

1. living in (town)?
2. teaching/learning English?
3. teaching at/going to this school?
4. driving a (name of car)/learning the (instrument)?

4 Listen to an interview with a rock band on tour.

Note down:
   how long they have been touring.
   how long they have been playing together.
   when they made their first record.
   what it was called.
   how they got their name.

5 Write a paragraph about the rock band in exercise 4 or about one of your favourite bands. Begin:

Genie are my favourite rock band. They have been playing together for/since …

Joke time!
MAN: I see you've been working in your garden for hours and hours. What are you growing?
WOMAN: Tired!

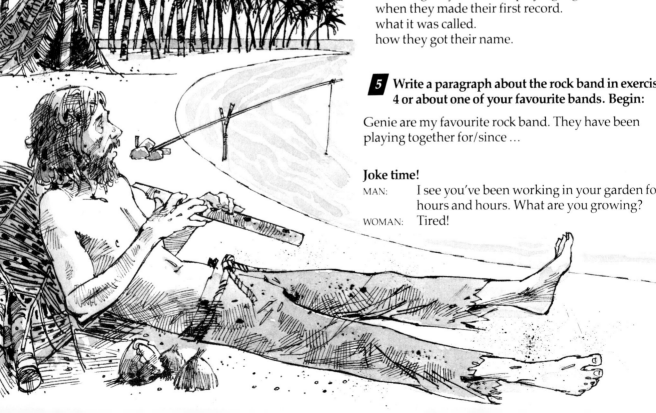

Race to the South Pole

🔊 Read and listen

In 1909, an Englishman, Robert Scott, went on an expedition to the South Pole. Scott and his companions didn't survive the return journey. Scott's diary was found beside his body.

16 or 17 March.

Things are getting worse. Two days ago, at noon, poor Titus Oates said he couldn't continue because of his leg. He asked us to leave him in his sleeping bag. We could not do that. We completed our afternoon march. At night he was worse, and we knew that the end was near. Oates' last thoughts were of his Mother. Hope never left him before the end. There was a wild snowstorm. He said 'I am just going outside. I may be some time.' He went out into the snowstorm, and we have not seen him since. We knew that poor Oates was walking away to die. It was an act of a brave man. We all hope to meet the end with this kind of courage – and surely death is not far away. We talk all the time of completing the trip. But I don't think any of us believes it in his heart.

1 Answer

1. Where were Scott and his companions returning from?
2. Why was it difficult for Oates to continue the journey?
3. What did Oates ask them to do?
4. What did they say?
5. Did Oates get better that night?
6. What was the weather like?
7. What did Oates say?
8. What did he do?
9. Did he come back?
10. Did Scott and his companions think they were going to get back safely?

Look!

'I can't continue,' he said.
He said (that) he couldn't
  continue.
'The end is near.'
We knew (that) the end was
  near.

After the verbs *say, know, hope*
  and *think*, the word *that* is
  optional.

2 Rewrite these sentences using the verbs in brackets.

1. 'I can't continue because of my leg.' (Oates/say)
   Oates said that he couldn't continue because of his leg.
2. 'You aren't in too much pain, I hope.' (Scott/hope)
3. 'I'm just going outside.' (Oates/say)
4. 'Oates is walking away to die.' (Scott/know)
5. 'Oates isn't coming back.' (Scott/know)
6. 'Oates is very brave.' (Scott/think)
7. 'The end is coming.' (Scott/know)

3 Join the words below to summarise what happened to Titus Oates.

Two days ago Titus Oates say/not continue/leg. Ask/leave/sleeping bag. Complete/afternoon march. Night/be worse. Know/end/near. Titus/walk out/snowstorm. Not/see/since.

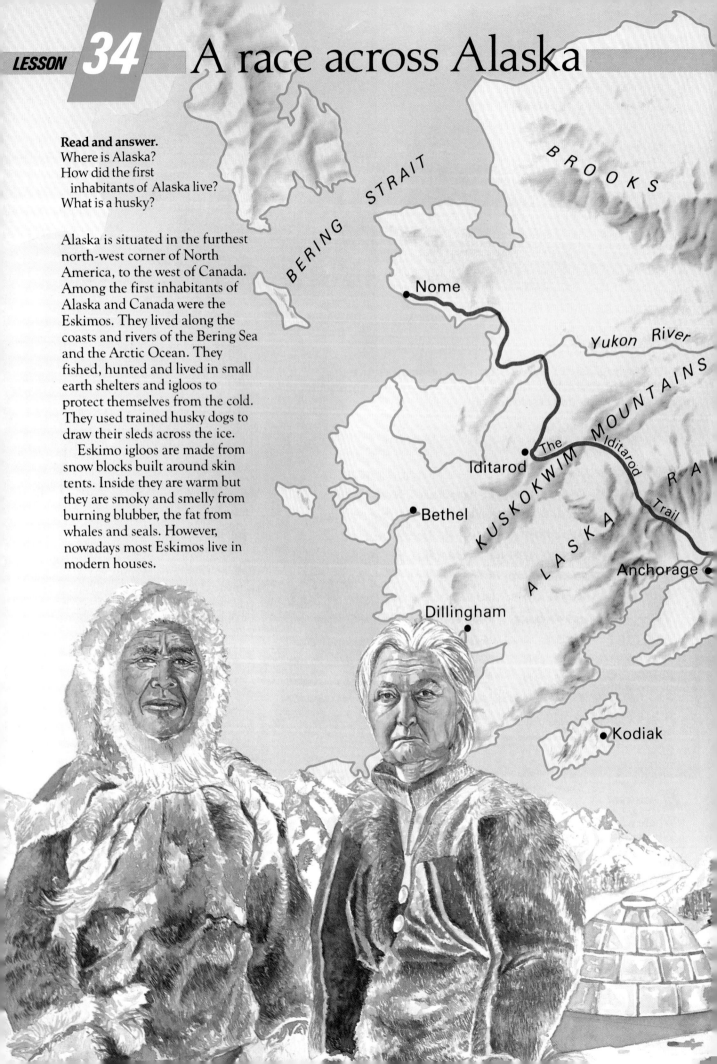

A race across Alaska

Read and answer.
Where is Alaska?
How did the first
  inhabitants of Alaska live?
What is a husky?

Alaska is situated in the furthest
north-west corner of North
America, to the west of Canada.
Among the first inhabitants of
Alaska and Canada were the
Eskimos. They lived along the
coasts and rivers of the Bering Sea
and the Arctic Ocean. They
fished, hunted and lived in small
earth shelters and igloos to
protect themselves from the cold.
They used trained husky dogs to
draw their sleds across the ice.

Eskimo igloos are made from
snow blocks built around skin
tents. Inside they are warm but
they are smoky and smelly from
burning blubber, the fat from
whales and seals. However,
nowadays most Eskimos live in
modern houses.

BERING STRAIT

BROOKS

Nome

Yukon River

KUSKOKWIM MOUNTAINS

The Iditarod Trail

Iditarod

Bethel

ALASKA RA

Anchorage

Dillingham

Kodiak

RANGE

E

The woman who won the world's toughest race

Libby Riddles, blonde, blue-eyed and tough as steel, has just won the most punishing race in the world.

In seventeen days she drove a dog team and sled across 1,050 miles of Alaska and through some of the most difficult terrain in the world. In bitter winds and snowstorms she drove her dogs along the Iditarod Trail, which runs from Anchorage to Nome, in temperatures that reached −100°F.

Libby is the first woman ever to win the race. 'I still can't believe it,' she said, hugging her thirteen wild-eyed husky dogs.

Duane Halverson, who came second, said: 'It sure hurts when a young woman is ahead of you. But it doesn't hurt for long. She deserved to win.'

1 Copy and complete these sentences.

1. Alaska is a territory which....
2. The first inhabitants of Alaska were Eskimos who ...
3. An igloo is a shelter which ...
4. Huskies are dogs which ...
5. The Iditarod Trail is a route which...
6. Libby Riddles is the woman who ...

2 Copy and complete these sentences. Use each of the prepositions in the box once only.

along	through	around	among
below	over	across	above

1. The aeroplane flew high ... the clouds.
2. You have to walk ... the bridge to get to the other side.
3. ... the pile of photographs she found one of her mother.
4. The fish swam just ... the surface of the water.
5. If you wrap this ... your ankle, it'll feel better.
6. He hurried ... the dark forest.
7. We flew right ... the Tower of London.
8. She walked carefully ... the edge of the cliff.

3 Discuss these questions in pairs or groups.

1. What do you like about cold weather?
2. What is the coldest temperature you have ever experienced?
3. What sort of things would you have in your igloo?

Did you know?
Eskimos use fridges to stop their food from freezing.

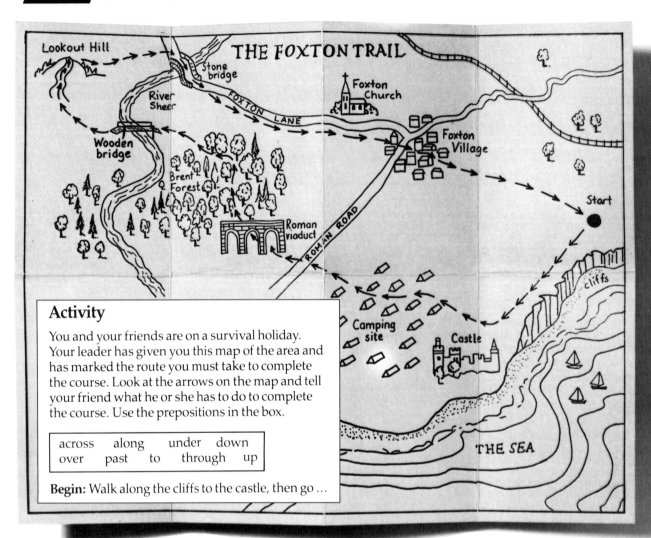

THE FOXTON TRAIL

Activity

You and your friends are on a survival holiday. Your leader has given you this map of the area and has marked the route you must take to complete the course. Look at the arrows on the map and tell your friend what he or she has to do to complete the course. Use the prepositions in the box.

across	along	under	down
over	past	to	through	up

Begin: Walk along the cliffs to the castle, then go ...

Roleplay

You are talking to a friend one Friday afternoon.

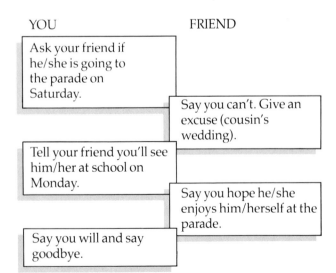

YOU	FRIEND
Ask your friend if he/she is going to the parade on Saturday.	
	Say you can't. Give an excuse (cousin's wedding).
Tell your friend you'll see him/her at school on Monday.	
	Say you hope he/she enjoys him/herself at the parade.
Say you will and say goodbye.	

Now write the dialogue.

🔊 Listen

Listen to this interview with Carol, who is studying modern dance. Answer the questions.

1. Where is she studying?
2. How long has she been studying there?
3. Where is she from?
4. How old is she?
5. How long has she been dancing?
6. What is her ambition?

Write

1. Report what Carol said about where she was studying , where she was from, her dancing career and her ambition.
2. Imagine you have left school and are now studying a special skill or subject. Write a paragraph about yourself.

Dictionary skills

Find these words in your dictionary. Write down each word and put the part of speech (*n, v, adj* or *adv*) beside it. Then write down the meaning in your own language.

1. courage   2. advise   3. surely   4. brave

Grammar Lessons 31-35

Modal have got to *(obligation)*

I've		visit my grandmother.
She's	got to	go an a course.
We've		cook our own food.
They've		build a shelter.

Reflexive pronouns

myself	ourselves
yourself	yourselves
himself	themselves
herself	

Present perfect continuous

How long	have you		been	living here? studying English?
	has	he she		

I've He's She's	been	living here learning English	since November. for three months.

I	haven't	been	living here studying English	long.
He She	hasn't			

Reporting verbs

He I	knew said thought hoped	(that)	he I	was	going to die. going outside. very brave.
				couldn't continue.	
				wasn't in too much pain.	

Prepositions of direction and position

She drove the dogs	along the trail. through the forest. across Alaska.

They flew	above below among	the clouds.
	over Alaska.	

It's kept in the safe.

SMUGGLERS DISCO ▲

MARGATE'S TOP DISCO

Smugglers' and Pirates' Night

Thursday from 9 pm

All the latest rock videos

on two gigantic screens

Admission £3

📼 Dialogue

JULIE: Thanks for coming to help us.

RICK: What exactly do you want me to do?

JULIE: Take the money at the door and play the videos for the disco.

RICK: Fine.

JULIE: The cash box is kept in the safe in my office.

RICK: Right. Where can I put my things?

JULIE: In the room behind the bar. It's where the drinks are stored but it's also used as a staff cloakroom.

RICK: Have I got to wear a costume like the others?

JULIE: I'm afraid so. We all wear costumes on special nights. But don't worry, you'll look terrific in an eyepatch!

> **Look!**
> We keep the cash box in the safe.
> = The cash box is kept in the safe.
> The staff use this room.
> = This room is used by the staff.

1 Answer.

1. What does Julie want Rick to do?
2. Where is the cash box kept?
3. Where can Rick leave his things?
4. What is stored in the room behind the bar?
5. Who is the room also used by?
6. When are costumes worn by the staff?

2 Ask and answer about your school.

A: Who uses this room?

B: This room is used by Class 4A.

1. Who uses this room?
2. Who cleans the classrooms?
3. Who types the head teacher's letters?
4. Who marks your biology exams?
5. Where do you perform school plays?
6. Where do they store the textbooks?

4 **Discuss some of the following questions:**

1. What sort of fruit is grown in your country?
2. Is any wine produced in your country? Where?
3. Where are the latest films shown near you?
4. Where are pop concerts held near you?
5. Where is the best icecream sold?
6. Where are the best clothes shops situated?

5 **Roleplay**

On the telephone, invite a friend to come with you to Smugglers Disco next Thursday.

YOU | FRIEND

Answer the phone.

Greet your friend and say who you are. Ask what he/she is doing next Thursday evening.

Ask why.

Say you want to go to Smugglers Disco.

Ask why Thursday is such a special night.

Explain why and ask if your friend would like to come.

Ask how much it costs.

Say how much it costs.

Say you'll come and ask what your friend is going to wear.

Explain about the special costumes.

Ask what time it starts.

Say what time and arrange a time and place to meet.

3 **Use the words in the box to answer the questions.**

glass	leather	paper	water	potatoes
metal	cotton	nylon	cream	eggs
wood	wool	plastic	flour	milk

What are these things made of?
1. your desk or table.
2. your shoes.
3. your pen.
4. your T-shirt or shirt.
5. your classroom window.
6. your textbook.
7. your sweater.

What are these things made from?
1. butter.
2. an omelette.
3. ice.
4. chips.
5. crisps.
6. bread.

6 **Write a letter to a friend describing the evening you spent at Smugglers Disco. Say who you went with, what you wore, what the disco was like, who you met, how long you stayed and how you got home.**

Someone had taken it.

One day a few years ago a very funny thing happened to a neighbour of mine. He is a lecturer at one of London's big medical schools. He had finished his teaching for the summer term and was at the airport on his way to Rumania to give a lecture on anatomy.

He had packed a few clothes and his lecture notes in his hand luggage but he had put Rupert, the skeleton he uses in his lectures, in a large brown suitcase. At the check-in desk, he realised he had forgotten to buy a newspaper. He left his suitcase near the desk and went over to the kiosk.

When he got back he discovered that someone had taken his suitcase. He often wonders what they said when they opened it and found Rupert.

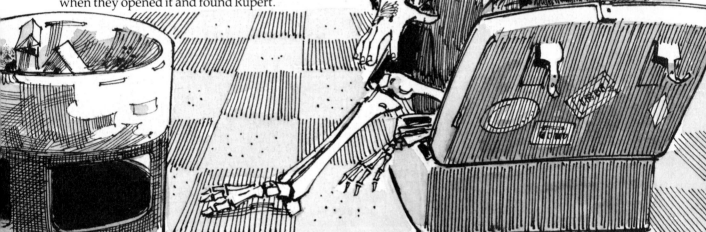

1 Write the events in the correct order.

1. He went to the airport.
2. While he was away, someone took his suitcase.
3. He finished his teaching for the summer term.
4. He left the suitcase near the check-in desk.
5. He packed Rupert, his skeleton, in a suitcase.
6. He went to buy a newspaper.

> *Look!*
>
> PAST SIMPLE
> Someone took his suitcase.
> He got back and discovered this.
>
> PAST PERFECT
> When he got back he discovered that someone had taken his suitcase.

2 In pairs, answer the questions.

1. Why was he free to go to Rumania?
   Because he had …
2. Where had he put Rupert?
3. Why did he go to the kiosk?
4. Where did he leave the suitcase?
5. What did he discover when he got back?

3 Write a dialogue between the lecturer and an airport policeman. The policeman wants to know where he left the suitcase, why, what it looks like, and what was in it.

LECTURER: Officer, someone has …
POLICEMAN: I see. Where did you leave it?

4 📼 Listen to Susan telling a similar story and answer these questions.

1. Where was Susan going?
2. How was she travelling?
3. How did the 'kind' man steal her suitcase?
4. What was in it?

5 Write a paragraph retelling Susan's story.

🎧 **Read and listen**

One afternoon John Trenchard, who is fifteen, by chance discovers a secret passage in the graveyard of the village of Moonfleet. Later that night he returns with a candle to explore the secret passage.

I kept in the shadows as I walked along the street. Everyone was asleep in Moonfleet, and there were no lights in any of the windows except the inn. When I reached the graveyard I began to feel afraid. I looked at the hole under the stone,
5 and I didn't know whether to go on or go back. Then, to my surprise, I saw a boat lying near the shore. It was strange for a boat to be in Moonfleet Bay so late at night. Then I saw a blue light on the boat and I knew it was the smugglers' boat and that they were
10 giving a signal to someone on the shore. I took one last look round and entered the hole.
   Holding my candle high up in front of me, I walked down the passage. At last I came to a stone wall which someone had built across the passage, but
15 which was now broken to make a door. I stood still and wondered what sort of place I had come to.
   I went through and found myself in a large room. In the middle of the room were a great number of boxes and barrels full of smuggled goods. I had found the
20 smugglers' storeroom!

1 Answer.

1. Why did John need a candle?
2. Why did he think that everyone in the village was asleep?
3. Why did he know that the boat in the harbour belonged to the smugglers?
4. How did he know he had found the smugglers' storeroom?

> *Look!*
> When I reached the graveyard, I began to feel afraid.

2 Join these sentences with when.

1. He returned to the graveyard. He had a candle with him.
2. He saw the hole. He didn't know what to do.
3. He saw the wall across the passage. He stood still.
4. He entered the room. He found a large number of boxes.

3 Write complete sentences to make a summary of the text.

1. One night/John Trenchard/decide/explore/secret passage/graveyard/Moonfleet.
2. When/reach graveyard/feel afraid.
3. Then/see boat/Moonfleet Bay.
4. Know/smugglers' boat/blue light.
5. Enter hole/walk down passage/until/come to a door in wall.
6. When/go through/find room/boxes and barrels/ smuggled goods.
7. Suddenly/know find/smugglers' storeroom.

4 Find the odd word in each group.

1. bay   beach   road   shore
2. wall   floor   boat   door
3. hotel   hospital   inn   restaurant
4. candle   box   barrel   packet
5. asleep   afraid   frightened   terrified

Joke time!
What did the boy octopus say to the girl octopus?
I want to hold your hand, hand, hand, hand, hand, hand, hand, hand.

Read and answer.

Why are pop videos important?

What are they like?

Where are a lot of them made?

In the United States they're called 'clips'. In Britain they're called 'promos' or 'pop videos'. These are the videos which can make a pop record into a success or a failure.

　　For several years now, London has been the best place to go if you want to make a pop video. For a pop singer today, the video is often as important as the music. Pop videos are really like advertisements. They are used to promote and sell records and are therefore a very important part of the record business.

　　There are two kinds of pop video. One is called a 'performance' video. This is a video where the performers play and sing their song. The other is called a 'conceptual' video, where the music is played in a strange or exotic setting – like a cave, old docks or a tropical island.

　　Although they last only about four to five minutes, these mini-films are not cheap to make. Recently a new band made a video in London. There were thirty people working on it including eleven actors and a pony! These people worked all night in an empty warehouse. The video cost £50,000 to make but the record only reached number 147 and then disappeared from the charts.

1 Write questions for these answers.

1. They're called 'clips'.
2. London.
3. Because they promote and sell records.
4. 'Performance' and 'conceptual'.
5. A video where the performers play and sing.
6. About four to five minutes.
7. No, they're expensive.

The Week	Last Week	Weeks on Chart	Description (tracks) Timings/Rec. Retail Price	
1	1	59	**DIRE STRAITS: Alchemy Live** Live (10 tracks)/1hr 20min/£9.99	Channel 5 CFV 001 22
2	NEW		**DIANA ROSS: The Visions Of Diana Ross** Compilation (6 tracks)/30min/£9.99	PMI MVR 99 0049 2
3	18	2	**HITS 4 VIDEO SELECTION** Compilation (14 tracks)/55 min/£9.99	RCA/Columbia RVT 10919
4	7	9	**TALKING HEADS: Stop Making Sense** Live (19 tracks)/1hr 39min/£19.95	Palace/PMI PVC 3010M
5	3	15	**MADONNA: The Virgin Tour** Live (10 tracks)/50min/£19.95	WEA Music K 9381053
6	6	3	**VIDEO HITS 2** Compilation (14 tracks)/56 min/£6.99	Wienerworld/Video Collection VC 4007
7	4	29	**KATE BUSH: The Single File** Compilation (12 tracks)/50 min/£14.99	PMI MVP 99 1031 2
8	20	2	**DURAN DURAN: The Making Of Arena** Behind The Scenes/50 min/£14.95	PMI MVP 99 1117 2
9	12	2	**THE STYLE COUNCIL: The Video Singles** Compilation (4 tracks)/16 min/£7.99	Channel 5 CFV 00282
10	24	2	**ROXY MUSIC: The High Road** Live (14 tracks)/1 hr 15 min/£9.99	Channel 5 CFV 00012
11	5	5	**JOHN LENNON: Live In New York City** Live (14 tracks)/55 min/£14.95	PMI MVP 99 1115 2
12	7	14	**WHAM!: Wham '85** EP (3 tracks)/19 min/£9.99	CBS/Fox 3075 50
13	9	44	**QUEEN: Live In Rio** Live (16 tracks)/1hr/£14.99	PMI MVP 99 1079-2
14	16	3	**FLEETWOOD MAC: Mirage Tour** Live (13 tracks)/80 min/£9.99	Channel 5 CFV 00032
15	9	91	**U2: Live "Under A Blood Red Sky"** Live (12 tracks)/61min/£19.95	Virgin/PVG VVD 045
16	11	2	**DIO: Live In Concert** Live (8 tracks)/1hr/£9.99	Channel 5 CFV 00142
			...TRY: Live	Channel 5 CFV 00232

Music and

Look!
This is a video where performers play and sing their song.

2 **Rewrite these sentences using** where.

1. He took the leading part in this film.
   This is the film where ...
2. I keep all my old pop magazines in this cupboard.
3. We watch television in this room.
4. Mick Jagger and David Bowie performed together in this video.
5. All the stars gave their performances free in this concert.

3 **Find the odd word in each group.**

1. guitar   drum   lead singer   piano
2. orchestra   backing group   pop band   record
3. cave   docks   warehouse   video
4. advertisement   amplifier   loudspeaker   microphone

4 **In a group discuss your favourite and least favourite videos.**

I like ...'s latest video.
I especially like the bit where ...
I can't stand ...

5 **Write a paragraph describing your favourite video.**

Write about:
   who the performers are.
   where it is set.
   what sort of things the performers do.

My favourite video at the moment is by a group called China Crisis and it's called ... It is set in a ... and they sing while they ...

Roleplay

Your friend Shane has written to 'Top of the Pops', a TV pop music programme, to ask if you can both be part of the audience. Use Shane's notes about the arrangements to roleplay a conversation.

> Tickets to join audience for 'Top of the Pops'.
> Broadcast : August 17th
> Report at studio entrance at 5 pm.
> Costumes provided.
> No pay but given hot meal and taxi fare home.

YOU	SHANE
Ask if Shane has heard from 'Top of the Pops' yet.	
	Reply and say when it is.
Ask what time you've got to report at the studio on the day.	
	Give the information.
Ask if you can wear your own clothes.	
	Reply and explain.
Ask if you get paid.	
	Reply and explain about meal and taxi.
Say goodbye and arrange to meet outside studio.	
	Agree and say goodbye.

Word study

Rewrite the sentences. Replace the expressions with 'put' with the correct form of one of the verbs below.

> to cover (with)   to dress (in)   to build   to hide
> to place   to support   to fix (to something)

1. She didn't want her brother to see his birthday present so she *put* it *in a place where he wouldn't find it.*
2. The flowers were so beautiful that he *put* them in the middle of the room where everyone could see them.
3. As it was a fancy dress party, we all *put on* some funny clothes.
4. As they were going to paint the room, they *put* old newspapers *on* the floor.
5. He *put* the notice firmly *on* to a tree with a nail.
6. As the house was on the edge of a forest, they *put up* a fence to keep out the wild animals.
7. As the box was not very strong, he *put his hands under* the bottom of it while she lifted it.

📼 Listen

Listen to a special effects technician from a film studio describing how the actors who play people like Superman, Supergirl and Santa Claus are made to fly. Copy and complete the paragraph using the correct form of the verbs.

cover	film	dress	project	build
hide	place	support	fix	attach

First the Niagara Falls are … from a helicopter. A wall … and this … with a great big screen. Then the actor … in a steel waistcoat which … by his or her costume. The waistcoat … to a horizontal steel bar which … securely to the wall about 50 metres high. Lots of mattresses … underneath in case the actor falls. The background film of the Niagara Falls … on to the screen and filmed again, this time with the actor in place. Now the actor appears to be flying over Niagara Falls.

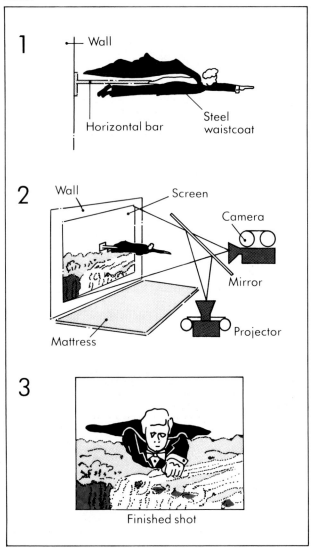

1   Wall
Horizontal bar   Steel waistcoat

2   Wall   Screen   Camera   Mirror   Projector   Mattress

3   Finished shot

Write

Use the outline below to write a story called 'Mr Pickford's surprise'.

It was 7.45 on a Monday morning and Mr Pickford, manager at Heston Biscuit factory, yawned as he left home to go to work.
Describe what he had done at the weekend.
He went to his office and opened the door. To his amazement he found a lion facing him.
Describe what the lion was doing.
Say what Mr Pickford did.
Explain how the lion had got there.

Dictionary skills

Find these words in your dictionary and note which four are spelt wrongly.

1. skelleton   3. suitcase   5. smuggle
2. texbook   4. forgotton   6. bisiness

Grammar Lessons 36-40

Present passive

| Where | is the money | kept? |
| | are the textbooks | stored? |

| The money is kept in the safe. |
| The books are stored in those cupboards. |

| A table | is made | of wood. |
| Butter | | from milk. |

Past perfect in contrast with past simple

| He had | finished teaching for the summer term | and was at the airport. |
| | packed his skeleton in his suitcase | |

| He realised | he | had forgotten to buy | a paper. |
| | | hadn't bought | |
| When he got back, someone had taken his suitcase. |

Reported speech with know

I knew (that)	it was the smugglers' boat.
	they were giving a signal.
	I had found the smugglers' storeroom.

Defining relative clause with where

| This is a video | where | the performers play and sing. |
| I like the bit | | he sings on a tropical island. |

You'd better watch it!

🔊 Dialogue

One morning, Rick is late for work at AIP. Tony, his boss, is angry.

TONY: Andrea, where's Rick? It's past ten o'clock. I want him to deliver this parcel urgently.

ANDREA: He hasn't come in yet. Perhaps he's ill or something.

TONY: This isn't the first time he's been late. You'd better go with the parcel instead.

ANDREA: Here he is now.

RICK: Hi folks! Sorry I'm late. I had a puncture.

TONY: Well, you'd better not be late again!

RICK: What's the matter with him? He's very sour today.

ANDREA: You'd better watch it, Rick. You'll get the sack if you're not careful.

1 **Copy and complete this conversation between Andrea and her boyfriend, Chris.**

CHRIS: Did anything exciting happen at work today?

ANDREA: Well, Rick got into trouble with Tony.

CHRIS: Really? Why?

ANDREA: ....

CHRIS: Why? Did he oversleep?

ANDREA: ....

CHRIS: Poor man! I know what it's like. I had a puncture last week. Was Tony angry?

ANDREA: ....

CHRIS: But it was an accident! He's not late every day, is he?

ANDREA: ....

CHRIS: What do you think will happen if he's late again?

ANDREA: ....

> *Look!*
> You'd better go without him.
> You'd better not be late again.
> We'd better hurry.

2 **Give advice or warnings in these situations using** you'd/we'd better (not)**.**

A: I've got an awful headache.

B: You'd better take an aspirin.

1. I've got an awful headache.

2. We're going to miss the bus if we don't hurry.

3. I'm sorry I'm late. I didn't have a watch on me.

4. I don't know where we are. I think we're lost.

5. I'm sorry I haven't done it. I forgot.

6. Look! There's someone suspicious outside that jeweller's shop.

3 **Match the apologies with suitable explanations. Write each apology in full with a response.**

A: I'm sorry I'm late. I missed the bus.
B: That's all right.

1. I'm sorry I'm late.   I left my books at school.
2. I'm sorry I didn't write.   My alarm clock wasn't
3. I'm sorry I didn't do my   working.
   homework.   I missed the bus.
4. I'm sorry I broke the   I lost your address.
   vase.   I knocked it over by
5. I'm sorry I overslept.   accident.

4 **Write advice.**

Because your bike lights aren't working, you accidentally cycle into the back of your neighbour's parked car and break a light on the car. You immediately tell your parents. Write five things which your parents might say to you, using *you'd better*.

You'd better go and apologise…

> **Look!**
> This is(n't) the first time he's been late.

5 **Imagine you are doing things for the first time. Comment on your experiences.**

This is the first time I've been to London.

1. go to London.
2. do any waterskiing.
3. ride on a donkey.
4. eat octopus.
5. be in helicopter.
6. have an accident.
7. win a prize.

6 **Roleplay this conversation. You are staying with an English family in Dover. On the first morning you oversleep and are late for breakfast.**

Apologise and explain why you are late.
The mother/father is not angry but warns you not to oversleep tomorrow because your group is leaving early to go to Brighton.

7 **Now write the conversation.**

It might be chocolates.

One morning, there was a ring at the door.
'That must be the postman,' said Kate, 'I know
his whistle'. She went to open the door.
'It's for your mother,' said the postman.
Kate took the parcel into the kitchen and put it on
the table.
'It might be from Gran,' she said. 'She often
sends us parcels.'
Andy looked at the stamps.
'It can't be,' he said. 'It's from Holland.'
Kate looked at the postmark.
'On the other hand, it could be from Cindy. She's
in Europe. It's probably chocolates,' she added,
feeling the parcel, which was in the shape of a
box.
'Mmm, I'd love one right now!' said Andy, 'Mum
won't mind if we open it.'
At that moment, Mrs Morgan came into the
kitchen.
'Oh good!' she said. 'My tulip bulbs from
Amsterdam have arrived! Perhaps you two
would like to help me plant them.'

Look!

It	can't be from Gran.
	might be from Cindy.
	could be chocolates.
	must be the postman.

1 Be a detective. Cover the text and answer the
questions.

1. Why did Kate think that the person at the door was
   the postman?
2. Who was the parcel for?
3. Why did Kate think it might be from their
   grandmother?
4. How did Andy know it wasn't from her?
5. Why did Kate think it could be from Cindy?
6. Why did Kate think it might be chocolates?
7. What was in the box?

2 Look at the pictures and say what you think they
could be.

A: I think it could be a …
B: Or it might be a …

3 Look at these two people. Build a possible
picture of their lives and backgrounds.

Make suggestions about:
    what their ages might be.
    what their jobs might be.
    what their families and home lives might be like.

A: I think he looks about sixty. On the other hand, he
   might be younger.
B: He certainly looks over fifty.

4 Guess the meaning.

What is a *corroboree?*
Is it:
    an African snake?
    an Australian aboriginal dance?
    a West Indian dish?
    a Tibetan sword?

5 📼 Listen to these scenes. Say where you think
they might be and why.

Joke time!
GIRL: Why are you wearing only one glove?
BOY: Because the weather forecast said it might be
        cold, but on the other hand it might be warm.

The golden glasses

📼 Read and listen

Sherlock Holmes, the famous detective, is investigating a murder. A police detective, Hopkins, has found a pair of glasses beside the body. Dr Watson, Holmes' assistant, tells the story.

He gave Holmes the pair of glasses. Holmes took them and looked at them carefully. After a few minutes he took a piece of paper and wrote something on it. Then he gave it to Hopkins. Hopkins read the note.

'Try to find a woman who has plenty of money and wears good clothes. She has
5   a thick nose, and her eyes are close together. She stares when she looks at things. She has visited an optician at least twice during the last two months. Her glasses are unusually strong and rather expensive. There are not many good opticians in London so I think you can find her easily.'

The detective was surprised when he read this, and so was I. Holmes
10   laughed. He said:

'Glasses can tell us many things about people. These must belong to a woman; they are very pretty. She must have money and like good things because the glasses are made of gold. And you can tell about her nose and eyes from the shape of her glasses.'

15   'But what about her staring, and the visits to the optician?' I asked.
Holmes replied: 'People with bad eyes always stare when they look at things. I saw that the glasses had been mended twice, at different times. The gold is very new and yellow in one place, in the other it is a little older.'

'You are so clever, Holmes,' I said.
20   'Elementary, my dear Watson,' he replied.

1 Which is correct?

1. Holmes knew the glasses belonged to a woman because
   a) they were expensive.
   b) they were attractive to look at.
2. Holmes knew the woman was rich because
   a) the glasses were made of gold.
   b) the glasses came from a well-known London optician.
3. Holmes knew the woman stared because
   a) she was a rude person.
   b) she had bad eyesight.
4. Holmes knew she had been to an optician twice because
   a) he saw the appointments in her diary.
   b) her glasses had been mended twice.

2 Copy and complete the sentences below using the words in the box once only.

> stare at   look at   look for   see   watch

1. Can you help me to ... my glasses? I can't find them anywhere.
2. How often do you ... television?
3. Please don't ... people, Lucy. It's rude.
4. ... this old school photograph. Can you ... where I am?

3 Be a detective. A man booked into a five-star hotel in London under the name of John Smith and left seven days later without paying his bill. The police are trying to trace him.

You go to the hotel room and find these items:
  a bow tie.
  an opera programme.
  a glass and an empty bottle of champagne.
  a spectacle case.
  an electric razor with an adaptor.
  an old-fashioned brown suitcase.
  a few dollar bills.
  a telephone number written on the top left-hand side of the mirror in felt tip pen.

What do these items tell you about the missing person? Write a note to the policeman in charge.

Try to find a man who ...

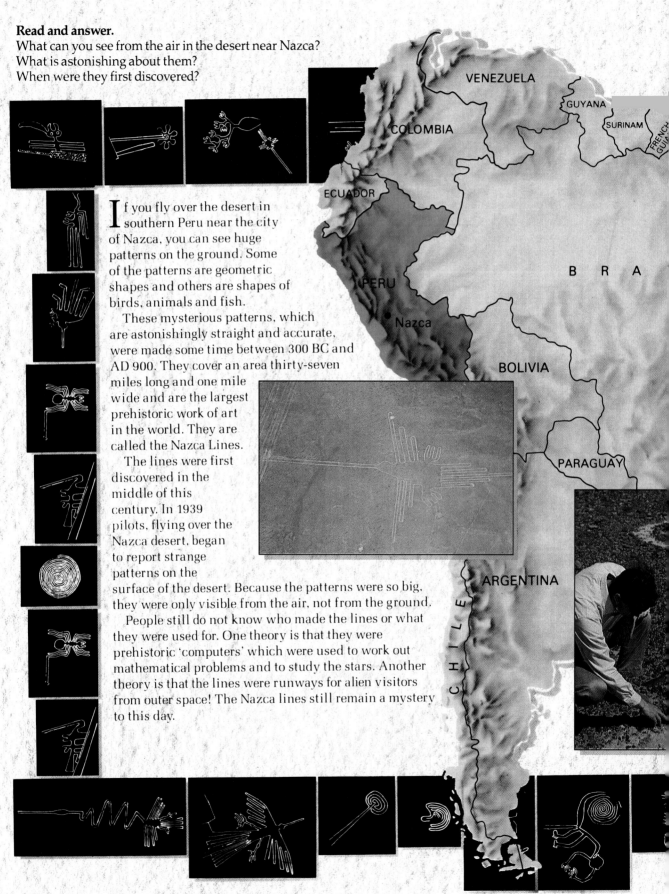

Read and answer.
What can you see from the air in the desert near Nazca?
What is astonishing about them?
When were they first discovered?

I f you fly over the desert in southern Peru near the city of Nazca, you can see huge patterns on the ground. Some of the patterns are geometric shapes and others are shapes of birds, animals and fish.

These mysterious patterns, which are astonishingly straight and accurate, were made some time between 300 BC and AD 900. They cover an area thirty-seven miles long and one mile wide and are the largest prehistoric work of art in the world. They are called the Nazca Lines.

The lines were first discovered in the middle of this century. In 1939 pilots, flying over the Nazca desert, began to report strange patterns on the surface of the desert. Because the patterns were so big, they were only visible from the air, not from the ground.

People still do not know who made the lines or what they were used for. One theory is that they were prehistoric 'computers' which were used to work out mathematical problems and to study the stars. Another theory is that the lines were runways for alien visitors from outer space! The Nazca lines still remain a mystery to this day.

VENEZUELA
GUYANA
SURINAM
FRENCH GUIANA
COLOMBIA
ECUADOR
B R A
PERU
Nazca
BOLIVIA
PARAGUAY
ARGENTINA
CHILE

69

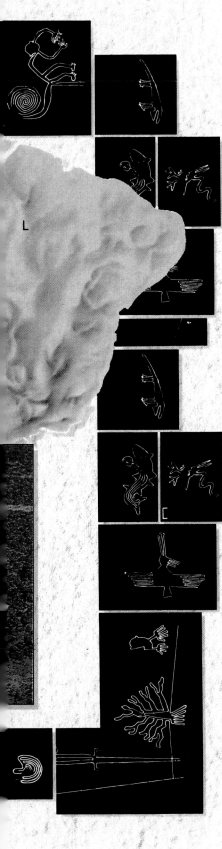

> **Look!**
> When were the Nazca lines discovered?
> They were discovered in 1939.

1 Write out these questions in full. Answer the questions and use the answers to write a summary of the text.

1. When/Nazca lines/made?
2. When/they/discovered?
3. From where/they/seen?
4. What/some people think/used for?

2 You are one of the pilots who first saw the Nazca lines. In pairs, complete this radio conversation with the control tower at Nazca.

YOU: ZX3 calling.
CONTROL: Come in ZX3! What is your position? Over.
YOU: ………
CONTROL: What can you see? Over.
YOU: ………
CONTROL: What are they like? Over.
YOU: ………
CONTROL: Animals! How big are they? Over!
YOU: ………
CONTROL: Have you an idea what they might be? Over!
YOU: ………
CONTROL: Well, you'd better report back to base immediately.

3 Use the verbs in the box and notes in the chart below to ask and answer about important historical events.

A: When was the tomb of Tutenkhamun discovered?
B: In 1922.
A: Where was it discovered?
B: In Luxor in Egypt.

| discover fight hold build invent run launch |

EVENT	PLACE/PEOPLE	DATE
The tomb of Tutenkhamun	Luxor, Egypt	1922
The Battle of Hastings	Sussex, England	1066
The 1984 Olympic Games	Los Angeles	
The Eiffel Tower	Paris	1889
The telephone	United States by Alexander Graham Bell	1876
The first modern Marathon race	Athens	1896
The first spacecraft	by the Russians	1957

4 Make remarks about the events to a partner:

Did you know that the tomb of Tutenkhamun was discovered in Luxor, Egypt in 1922?
Yes, I knew that./No, I didn't know that.

Now write a sentence about each event.
The Battle of Hastings was fought in Sussex in England in 1066.

Read and complete

Complete the newspaper article with the past passive form of the verb in brackets.

Last week treasure worth over £1 million (discover) off the Florida coast. The discovery (make) by a young British teenager, 17-year-old John Innes, who was on holiday with his family.

The treasure, which consists of gold coins and jewels, (find) in the wreck of a ship which experts believe (sink) by the famous pirate, Captain Kidd, in 1696.

John Innes was scuba diving near a small island off the Florida coast when he suddenly found the wreck of an old ship at the bottom of the sea. The coast guards (tell) immediately about the discovery and the treasure (bring) to the surface by a team of divers.

The coins and jewels, which officially belong to the US government, (examine) by archaeologists and (say) to be 'the real thing'. Yesterday at a press conference in Key West, John (give) a $1,000 reward for his school. When he (ask) if he was pleased with his reward, he replied: 'I'd rather have a bit of treasure!'

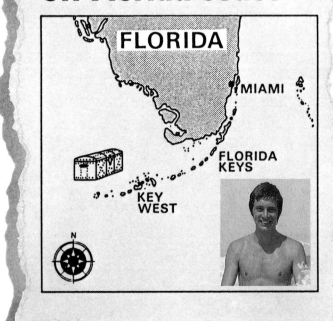

Startling discovery off Florida coast

Now write a conversation between a journalist and John on his return to Britain.

Roleplay

You are going out with your parents this evening and you promised to be back at 6 o'clock. You get back at 6.45 pm and they are angry. Roleplay the conversation.

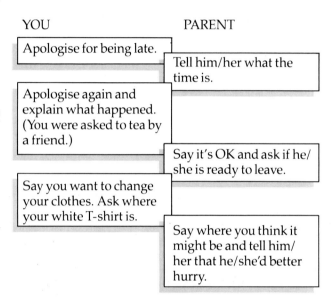

YOU

Apologise for being late.

Apologise again and explain what happened. (You were asked to tea by a friend.)

Say you want to change your clothes. Ask where your white T-shirt is.

PARENT

Tell him/her what the time is.

Say it's OK and ask if he/she is ready to leave.

Say where you think it might be and tell him/her that he/she'd better hurry.

Now write your conversation.

🔲 Listen

Listen to the next part of the Sherlock Holmes story 'The Golden Glasses'.
Sherlock Holmes thinks the person who murdered Mr Smith must be the woman with the golden glasses. Holmes goes to the house and finds a mark on a cupboard door in the room where Mr Smith was murdered. He decides to talk to the cook, Mrs Marker, about it.

Listen and choose the correct answers.
1. The 'mark' was made by
   a) a knife.
   b) a key.
   c) a lock.
2. Holmes thinks the person who made the mark was
   a) the cook, Mrs Marker.
   b) Mr Smith.
   c) the woman with the glasses.
3. Holmes thinks the woman with the glasses killed Mr Smith
   a) with a knife.
   b) with something from the cupboard.
   c) by pushing him on the floor.

Write

Write a letter to your penfriend:
apologise for not writing earlier and explain why.
say you would like to come and visit him/her.
say when you think you might be able to come but say he/she had better not plan anything special yet.
ask him/her to write soon.

Dear ...,
    I am sorry I haven't ...

Project

Find out about some important historical events in your country. Write about:

a famous battle.   a famous discovery.
a famous building.   a famous sporting event.
a famous invention.

Dictionary skills

Find the word HEAD in your dictionary. Note that *head* forms the first part of many other words, e.g. *headband, headphone.*
Find a word beginning with *head* which means:
1. a pain in the head.
2. the title at the top of a piece of writing.
3. the main point in the news as read on radio or TV.
4. the office or place where people work who control a large organisation.

Game

Make as many words as you can from the name SHERLOCK HOLMES.

■ Grammar Lessons 41-45

Modal had better

You'd / had better	go without him. watch it. not be late again.

Apologies

I'm sorry	I'm late. I didn't write.

Present perfect with first/second time

This is(n't) the first time	I've been to London. he's been late.

Probability

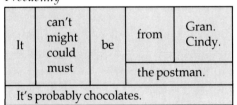

It's probably chocolates.

Past passive

When	were the Nazca lines discovered? was the Eiffel Tower built?

They were discovered in 1939.

It was built in 1889.

I wish he didn't.

📼 Dialogue

DEBBIE: Look! That boy outside the bike shop is staring at us.

KATE: Oh, no. Not him again. Quick, let's go into the chemist's.

DEBBIE: Who is he?

KATE: He's called Kevin Rowntree and he's always following me around. It really annoys me.

DEBBIE: Are you going out with him?

KATE: No! He's horrible! I met him at a school disco. I only danced with him once.

DEBBIE: Does he live near you?

KATE: Yes he does, in the same street, worse luck! I wish he didn't. I wish he lived in Timbuktu!

DEBBIE: Tell him to leave you alone.

KATE: I have! But he doesn't take any notice!

1 **Answer.**

1. Why does Debbie notice Kevin?
2. Where do Debbie and Kate go to avoid Kevin?
3. Does Kate like him?
4. Why does Kevin annoy her?
5. Where did she meet him?
6. What happens when Kate tells Kevin to leave her alone?

SECRET WISHES

Everyone wishes now and then that they could change a few things about their life. We'd like you to fill in our questionnaire and send it in.

Name: *Martina*   Age: *15*

Things you can't do very well: **Things you haven't got:**
draw   *a 3-speed bike*
dance   *a dog or a cat*
play the guitar   *a good camera*
speak English   *my own TV*

Things you don't like about yourself: **Things you want to change about your life:**
straight hair   *I don't get enough pocket money.*
braces on my teeth   *I have to walk to school.*
a birthmark on my arm   *I'd like an older sister or brother.*
big feet   *I'd like my own room.*
I'm not very tall.   *I'd like to be allowed to go out*
I'm not very good at sports.   *more in the evenings.*
                                      I'd like to live in the country.

2 Read the questionnaire completed by Martina and use her answers to imagine what she wishes she could change about her life and her looks.

She wishes she could draw well.
She wishes she had a 3-speed bike.
She wishes she didn't have straight hair.
She wishes she got more pocket money.

3 Tell your partner what you would like to change about your life.

4 Write a dialogue. You are feeling angry.

Your father asks what the matter is.
You say you've got too much homework to do each night and wish you had more free time.
Your father says you have to do homework if you go to school.
You say you wish…

74

'I'm so bored and lonely at home. The problem is that there is never anyone at home to talk to. My mother is always out working or doing something else. Sometimes I go to stay at a friend's house for a day or two, but when I come home again I feel even worse. I hate school holidays because I get fed up.'
Chris, Oxford

Dear Chris,
I am sorry to hear about your problem. If I were you, I would tell your mother exactly how you feel. She may have no idea that you are lonely. However, she is obviously busy and she probably doesn't have much time to spend with you. I think it would be a good idea if you had a new hobby. If you joined a club of some sort, you wouldn't be so lonely and bored and you would find it easier to make new friends.

1 Chris's aunt comes to see him. In pairs, complete their conversation.

AUNT: What's the matter, Chris? You look miserable.
CHRIS: ……… .
AUNT: Why?
CHRIS: ……… .
AUNT: Isn't your mother at home when you get back from school?
CHRIS: ……… .
AUNT: Don't you ever go and stay with a friend?
CHRIS: ……… .
AUNT: Well, that's fun, isn't it?
CHRIS: ……… .
AUNT: Never mind. The school holidays will soon be here!
CHRIS: ……… .

Look!
If I were you, I'd tell your mother.
If you had a new hobby, you wouldn't be so bored.

2 Look at the letter of advice and complete these sentences.

1. I … tell mother how you feel if I … you.
2. It … a good idea if you … a new hobby.
3. If you … a club, you … be so lonely.
4. You … so bored if you … a new hobby.
5. You … find it easier to make friends if you … a club.

3 In pairs, give advice in these different situations.

1. A friend of yours has lost an expensive watch at school.
   If I were you, I'd …
2. Your mother wakes up in the morning with a very bad cold and sore throat.
3. Your best friend wants to be a pop musician.
4. A friend of yours wants to go on a cheap holiday in Britain.
5. Your brother wants to take up martial arts.

4 In pairs or groups decide what you would do if you were bored and lonely like Chris.

Who would you talk to? What sort of club would you join? Would you write to a magazine about it? If so, which one?

5 🔲 Listen to this caller on a radio phone-in programme and make notes.

Note:
   the name of the caller.
   the problem.
   the advice which is given.

6 Write to a magazine telling them about someone you would most like to meet. Say who the person is, where you would go, what you would wear and what you would have to eat and drink.

Dear …,
      I would like to meet … . We would go to … and I would wear …

🔊 **Read and listen**

The Snow Goose

Philip Rhayader lived by himself in an old lighthouse at the mouth of a river where he painted and photographed birds. Philip was a hunchback. At first the village people were
5 afraid of him but they soon got used to him. However, no one found out that Philip was a kind and gentle man who loved all living creatures.

  One afternoon a girl came to the door. It
10 was November and Philip had been at the lighthouse for three years. The thought of knocking at the door filled her with fear. She had heard strange stories about the man who lived in the lighthouse. But the reason
15 she had come was more important than her fear: she had heard that this hunchback could make sick birds better.
  'What do you want, little girl?' he asked gently.
20 She pushed out her arms, which held a large white bird. There was blood on its feathers and on the front of her dress. She gave the bird to him.
  'I found it,' she said, so quietly that he could
25 hardly hear her.

'It's hurt. Is it still alive?'
'Yes. Yes, I think so,' he said, looking at it.
'Come in, child, come in.'

  The girl still felt afraid but she went in,
30 because she wanted to see inside the lighthouse. Philip put the bird on the table.
  'What kind of bird is it?' she said.
  'It's a snow goose from Canada,' he told her. Then he said to himself in surprise: 'I
35 wonder how it came here?'

---

1 **Answer.**

1. Where did Philip Rhayader live?
2. Why were people frightened of him?
3. What sort of person was he?
4. When did the girl come to see him?
5. Why did she want to see him?
6. What was she carrying in her arms?
7. What was the matter with it?
8. What sort of goose was it and where was it from?

2 **Write a summary of the text.**

Philip Rhayader was a .... who lived .... One afternoon in November, a girl came .... She was carrying .... which was still alive. Although she .... she had come because she had heard that .... Philip invited her .... He looked at the bird which was still .... and told her that it was ....

3 **You are the girl in the story. You have just come back from the lighthouse. Write a dialogue between you and your mother.**

Explain why you are late home for lunch.
Say where you have been and why you went there.

Joke time!
GIRL: You remind me of the sea.
BOY: Because I am wild, rough and romantic?
GIRL   No, because you make me sick!

My favourite magazine

Read and answer
Name five features you can find in *Streetbeat*.
Can you write to *Streetbeat* for a penfriend?

SPECIAL FEATURES

4 **Photostory**
The boy next door

8 **Quiz**
Have you got style?

12 **Special Offer**
The latest sportsbag from Sportac

14 **Competition**
Win £100 worth of new clothes from all branches of Teenwear.

HEALTH AND BEAUTY

16 **Fashion**
The complete holiday kit

18 **Hair**
Six new hairdos for him and her

19 **Make-up**
The latest tips on make-up for outdoor living

REGULAR FEATURES

21 **Problem Page**
Jo answers your problems.

23 **Penpal Column**
Penfriends galore for everyone

STREET BEAT!

- first in fashion and make-up
- tops for his and her hairstyles
- packed with posters, pop news and gossip
- full of sensational stories, fabulous free offers and competitions
- and . . . a penfriend column and a problem page

STREET BEAT!

1 Look at this list of magazine features. Choose eight of your favourite items. Put them down in the order in which you like to read them.

short stories	fashion advice	hobbies
photostories	problem page	cookery
sports news	make-up advice	cartoons
puzzles	careers guide	film reviews
competitions	pop gossip	shopping advice
news stories		

2 In groups, ask and answer about magazines.

Find out:
   which magazines people read.
   which ones are their favourites.
   which features they like reading best.
   which features they never read.

Tell the rest of the class about your group's top three magazines, top two features — and your least favourite feature! **Begin:**

The top three magazines which most people like are *Streetbeat*, *Ricky* and *Teenscene*. We all like problem letters but … . Not many people like … or … .

> *Look!*
>
> | We | could / should / ought to | have a problem page. |

3 Make a class magazine. Discuss and decide on eight features to include in your magazine. Write a contents list.

A: I think we ought to have a sports page.
B: OK. And we could have a fashion and make-up page too.
A: What about a competition? I think we should have a competition.
B: Yes. Let's have a pop music competition.

Choose a title for your magazine and write the articles.

4 📼 Listen to David talking about his work for a teenage magazine. He takes the photographs for photostories.

Note down:
   if he uses professional models.
   how he chooses the people to be photographed.
   what he tells them to do.

Imagine you are planning a trip to Britain.
Discuss:
  where to go, when and for how long.
  what you would like to see and do while you are
    there.
  how many hours a day you would like to study
    English.

Write

You are going to stay with Mr and Mrs Phillips while
you are in Britain. Write and tell them something
about yourself.

Write:
  your name, age and nationality.
  what you like doing in your spare time.
  what you'd like to do and see while you are there.
  about any food you don't like.

Discuss and write

In pairs, discuss what sort of things you need to take
with you, e.g. camera, raincoat, jeans. Make a list of
everything and compare your list with other people's.

🔊 Listen and discuss

You are now in Britain. It is Saturday morning and you
are not sure what to do at the weekend. Listen to the
telephone recording of 'London Information Line'.
Make notes of some of the things you can do. In
groups, discuss which sounds the most interesting or
exciting.

Write

Write a postcard to your parents or to a friend.
Tell them: how you are enjoying your holiday.
        what the weather and food is like.
        some of the things you have done and seen.

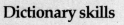

Discuss

In pairs, discuss your partner's suggestions for presents to take back home: one for your parents and one for your best friend.

Roleplay

Imagine you are in a shop. One of you is the customer, the other is the shop assistant. Buy the presents you have decided to get your parents and your friend.

A: Can I help you?
B: Yes, I'd like a ...
   Have you got a/any ...?
A: Yes. What sort/colour/size do you want?
B: ..., please. How much is it?
A: It's ...
B: I think I'll take it/this one, please.

Dictionary skills

You are doing a crossword and you have three words left to fill in. Read the clues and use your dictionary to help you find the answers.

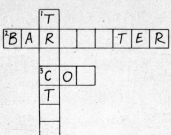

ACROSS
2. This will tell you what the weather is going to be like.
3. A baby sleeps in this.

DOWN
1. You drive one of these on a farm.

Grammar Lessons 46-50

I wish	I	was tall	but	I'm not.
		could waterski		I can't.
		had blue eyes		I haven't.
	he/she	lived in Timbuktu		he/she doesn't.
		didn't live here		he/she does.

Second conditional (if *clauses*)

If I were you, I'd tell your mother.
I'd tell your mother if I were you.
If you had a new hobby, you wouldn't be so bored.
You wouldn't be so bored if you had a new hobby.

Modal could (*suggestion*) should *and* ought to

We	could should ought to	have a problem page.

Oral exercises

1. Offer to do things
Oh dear. I haven't phoned the travel
agency yet.
Shall I phone them?
And I haven't got any foreign money.
Shall I get some?

1. phone
2. get
3. phone
4. tell
5. buy
6. write to

2. Make promises about a journey
Look after your luggage.
Don't worry. I'll look after my luggage.
Keep your passport safe.
Don't worry. I'll keep my passport safe.

1. Look after/luggage
2. Keep/passport safe
3. Keep/tickets/inside passport
4. Remember/change trains/Paris
5. Stay with/group
6. Remember/leave/address

3. Give information about your life
Do you live here?
Yes, I've lived here since 1985.
Are you at Castle Hill School?
*Yes, I've been at Castle Hill School for three
years.*

1. live/here/1985
2. be/Castle Hill School/three years
3. be/Class 3/September
4. know/Michael Roberts/1984
5. be/basketball team/last year

4. Give information about people
Have you heard the record?
*I've heard the record, but I haven't seen the
band.*
Has your sister seen the film?
*She's seen the film, but she hasn't read the
book.*

		Yes	No
1.	I	heard the record	seen the band
2.	She	seen the film	read the book
3.	We	seen the play	seen the film
4.	They	been to America	been to New York
5.	You	been to my house	met my parents
6.	He	visited Italy	been to Rome

5. Answer questions about you
(Open exercise)
Have you ever been abroad?
(Yes I have.)
Have your parents ever been abroad?
(No they haven't.)

1. Have you ever been abroad?
2. Have you parents ever been abroad?
3. Have you ever lived in a foreign
   country?
4. Have your parents ever lived in a
   foreign country?
5. Have you ever studied French?
6. Have you ever used a computer?

1. Give directions
How do I get there from London?
Which motorway do I take?
You take the M20 motorway.
Which exit do I turn off at?
You turn off at Exit 8.

LEEDS CASTLE

1. Take the M20 motorway.
2. Turn off at Exit 8.
3. Half a mile down the A20.
4. Turn right off the B2163.
5. Drive down the B2163
   for a few miles.
6. Follow the signposts for
   Leeds Castle.

1. How do I get there from London?
   Which motorway/take?
2. Which exit/turn off at?
3. How far/drive?
4. Where/turn right?
5. How far/drive down the B2163?
6. What/do then?

2. Make apologies
Can I speak to Jean, please?
I'm afraid she's just gone out.
Will you take this to the post office for
me?
*I'm afraid I've already been to the post office
today.*

1. speak to Jean/just gone out
2. take this/post office/already been/post
   office today
3. mended my bike/not finished it yet
4. borrow your radio/just lent it/Mark
5. not tell Sally/party/already/told her
6. ask Mark/my money/not see him yet

3. Give short answers
Has he just got home?
Yes, he has.
Have you already talked to him?
No, I haven't.

1. he/just got home/Yes
2. you/already talked to him/No
3. he/just come from Peter's house/Yes
4. they/already decided to leave/No
5. they/just told you about it/Yes
6. they/told their parents yet/No

4. Make comparisons (1)
Which is more interesting, playing
basketball or watching it?
*Playing basketball is more interesting than
watching it.*
Which is cheaper, going by bus or going
by train?
Going by bus is cheaper than going by train.

1. more interesting: playing basketball/
   watching it
2. cheaper: going by bus/going by train
3. easier: reading English/speaking it
4. more difficult: using a computer/using
   a calculator
5. cheaper: camping/staying in a hotel
6. more exciting: watching a horror film/
   watching a quiz show

5. Make comparisons (2)
(Open exercise)
Which is easier, reading English or
writing it?
(Reading English is easier than writing it.)
Which is more interesting, listening to
records or going to a concert?
*(Going to a concert is more interesting than
listening to records.)*

1. Which is easier, reading English or
   writing it?
2. Which is more interesting, listening to
   records or going to a concert?
3. Which is more fun, watching TV or
   going to the cinema?
4. Which is more difficult, studying a
   foreign language or studying Maths?
5. Which is more expensive, going to the
   cinema or going to the theatre?
6. Which is more dangerous, climbing
   mountains or hang-gliding?

LESSONS 11-15

1. Describe what people were doing

What was Helen doing when you saw her?
She was working.
And what were her parents doing?
They were sitting in the garden.

1. She/working
2. They/sitting in the garden
3. They/planning their holiday
4. She/having a rest
5. They/playing chess
6. He/having a shower

2. Ask for more information

Bernard was waiting outside the shop.
Who was he waiting for?
Susie was reading in the library.
What was she reading?

1. Bernard/waiting/Who?
2. Susie/reading/What?
3. Your parents/going/Where?
4. Princess Diana/wearing/What?
5. Mr Garret/driving/What?
6. Your mother/looking for/Who?

3. Check what people say

I was doing the washing-up when I heard the noise.
Sorry. What were you doing when you heard the noise?
They were sitting in the kitchen when they heard the noise.
Sorry. Where were they sitting when they heard the noise?

1. I/doing/washing-up
2. They/sitting/kitchen
3. Joseph/reading/paper
4. Marie/playing/garden
5. Mark and Ann/listening/records
6. I/sitting/in front of/house

4. Give opinions

Look at that cake!
It looks very nice.
What's the matter with the fish?
It smells horrible.

1. very nice
2. horrible
3. awful
4. delicious
5. wonderful
6. great

LESSONS 16-20

1. Answer personal questions

You're sixteen, aren't you?
Yes, I am.
You don't work here, do you?
No, I don't.

1. be sixteen/Yes
2. not work here/No
3. live in Dover/Yes
4. not lived there very long/No
5. want to go to university/Yes
6. not studying very hard/No

2. Check information

Your name's Simon Hall, isn't it?
Yes, it is.
You work at the safari park, don't you?
Yes, I do.

1. name/Simon Hall/Yes
2. work/safari park/Yes
3. haven't worked there very long/No
4. like working with animals/Yes
5. can't do all the jobs yet/No
6. don't know much about animals/No

3. Say how often you do things

How often do you go to school?
I go to school five times a week.
How often do you go to church?
I go to church once a week.

1. go/school/five times a week
2. go/church/once a week
3. go/youth club/three times a week
4. play/volleyball/twice a week
5. have to do/homework/four times a week
6. use/school computer/six times a week

4. Express a preference

Do you like walking to school?
I quite like walking to school, but I'd rather go by car.
Do you like living in this village?
I quite like living in this village, but I'd rather live in a town.

1. walking/school/go by car
2. living/village/live/town
3. travelling/by train/go by plane
4. working/shop/work/office
5. working/Mrs Williams/work/on my own
6. starting work/eight o'clock/start/half an hour later

5. Say what you like doing

(Open exercise)
Do you like sleeping in a tent?
(No, I don't.)
Do you like eating food in the open air?
(Yes, I do.)

1. Do you like sleeping in a tent?
2. Do you like eating food in the open air?
3. Do you like walking in the country?
4. Do you like cooking food over a fire?
5. Do you like camping with other people?
6. Do you like camping in cold weather?

LESSONS 21-25

1. Answer people's questions

Will it hurt?
Yes, I'm afraid it will.
Will it hurt a lot?
No, don't worry. It won't hurt a lot.

1. hurt/Yes
2. hurt a lot/No
3. take a long time/Yes
4. take more than two hours/No
5. be expensive/Yes
6. cost more than ten pounds/No

2. Talk about changes in your habits

Are you practising with a band?
No, I used to practise with a band, but I don't any more.
Oh. But you still like 'heavy metal', don't you?
No, I used to like 'heavy metal', but I don't any more.

1. practise with a band
2. like 'heavy metal'
3. like jazz
4. go to the opera
5. like music

3. Express polite surprise

We started work at six o'clock.
Really? Did you always use to start work so early?
And we worked ten hours a day.
Really? Did you always use to work so long?

1. start work/so early
2. work/so long
3. walk/so far
4. earn/so little
5. go to bed/so early

4. Talk about Mark's likes and dislikes
What does Mark think of smoking?
He can't stand smoking.
And eating junk food?
He doesn't mind eating junk food.

1. smoking/can't stand
2. eating junk food/doesn't mind
3. dogs/doesn't like
4. modern jazz/likes
5. visiting relations/can't stand
6. going on long car journeys/doesn't mind

5. Talk about your likes and dislikes
(Open exercise)
What do you think of smoking?
(I can't stand smoking.)

1. What do you think of smoking?
2. And eating junk food?
3. What do you think of dogs?
4. And modern jazz?
5. What about visiting relations?
6. And going on long car journeys?

LESSONS 26-30

1. Discuss the future
The band might be late.
Yes, what'll we do if the band's late?
The car might not come.
Yes, what'll we do if the car doesn't come?

1. band/late
2. car/not come
3. electrician/late
4. loudspeakers/not arrive on time
5. it/rain
6. lights/not work

2. Make decisions about the future
He may be in the office.
If he's in the office, we'll go and see him.
He may be busy.
If he's busy, we'll wait.

1. he/in the office/go/see him
2. he/busy/wait
3. he/in San Francisco/see him when he gets back
4. he/on holiday/talk to someone else
5. his wife/at home/go and see her
6. she/knows/what happened/find out from her

3. Make plans for the future
Maybe you won't pass your exams.
If I don't pass my exams, I'll take them again.
Maybe you won't get into university.
If I don't get into university, I'll look for a job.

1. not pass/exams/take them again
2. not get into university/look for a job
3. not find a job/go abroad and look for one
4. not have any money/borrow some from my parents
5. they/not lend me/money/borrow it from someone else
6. not like living abroad/come home again

4. Agree with people's advice
They should leave early, or they won't catch the train.
Yes, if they don't leave early, they won't catch the train.
They should make a reservation, or they won't get seats.
Yes, if they don't make a reservation, they won't get seats.

1. not leave early/not catch the train
2. not make a reservation/not get seats
3. not have passports/not get through customs
4. not have any foreign money/not be able to buy food
5. not book rooms/not have anywhere to stay
6. not talk to Mrs Cherry/not know the programme

5. Discuss people's chances of getting into the school football team
Is Mark in the team?
No. If he wants to be in the team, he should try harder.
How about Susan?
No. If she wants to be in the team, she should train more regularly.

1. he/try harder
2. she/train more regularly
3. he/run faster
4. she/practise more regularly
5. he/work harder
6. she/train more often

LESSONS 31-35

1. Say why people can't do things
Are you coming to the beach?
No. I've got to do the washing-up.
What about Simon?
No. He's got to make the beds.

1. I/washing-up
2. he/make the beds
3. she/clean the bathroom
4. he/tidy the sitting room
5. she/do the shopping
6. he/cook the dinner

2. Agree and give further information
Sheila lives here, doesn't she?
Yes, she's been living here for six years.
And her uncle lives here too.
Yes, he's been living here since 1986.

1. she/live here/six years
2. he/live/here/1986
3. she/work/there/three months
4. he/work/there/1985
5. she/study/there/last year
6. he/learn/German/a year and a half

3. Report what people said
'I'm going home.'
He said he was going home.
'It's raining.'
She said it was raining.

1. He/he/going home
2. She/it/raining
3. He/it/cold outside
4. She/she/going on holiday
5. He/he/leaving
6. She/it/terrible day

4. Give locations
Where's my suitcase?
It's in the cupboard.
Where's my purse?
It's on the television.

1. suitcase/in/cupboard
2. purse/on/television
3. shoes/under/bed
4. he/walking/across/road
5. diary/somewhere among/books on the desk
6. she/driving/along/road

LESSONS 36-40

1. Describe what normally happens

Do you keep the cash box in the safe?
Yes, the cash box is kept in the safe.
And do you use this room all the time?
Yes, this room is used all the time.

1. the cash box/keep/in the safe
2. this room/use/all the time
3. all the money/keep/in the cash box
4. the cash box/put/in the safe every night
5. the safe/lock/in the evenings
6. the back door/lock/too

2. Say where things come from

Where are these cassette recorders made?
They're made in China.
Where's this series produced?
It's produced in the USA.

1. cassette recorders/make/China
2. series/produce/USA
3. grapes/grow/Spain
4. cars/design/Italy
5. songs/record/Canada
6. computer/make/England

3. Talk about past events

Did you see Larry?
No, he had gone by the time I arrived.
Did you see the film?
No, it had finished by the time I arrived.

1. Larry/go
2. the film/finish
3. Sally's grandfather/go to bed
4. Sally's brother/leave
5. any food/everybody eat
6. Oliver/go home

4. Check what people say

Peter had put the briefcase in the kitchen.
Sorry? Where had he put the briefcase?
Mrs Hollins had given the money to Theresa.
Sorry? Who had she given the money to?

1. Peter/put/briefcase in the kitchen
2. Mrs Hollins/give/money to Theresa
3. They/leave/car by the river
4. They/give/keys to a boy
5. She/find/parcel in the park
6. She/give/it to a policewoman

LESSONS 41-45

1. Make apologies

I'm sorry I broke the glass. I didn't see it.
That's all right.
I'm sorry I'm late. I overslept.
That's OK.

1. break glass/not see it
2. late/oversleep
3. knock over the coffee/not see the cup
4. lose your umbrella/leave it on the bus
5. break the cup/drop it
6. break the video recorder/not know what happened

2. Respond to people's apologies

I'm sorry I knocked over the milk. Shall I clean it up?
Yes, please, if you could.
I'm sorry I broke your bike. Shall I mend it?
No, you'd better not. I'll mend it.

1. knock over/milk/clean it up/Yes
2. break/bike/mend it/No
3. lose/ticket/get another one/Yes
4. didn't give him/money/give it to him tomorrow/No
5. not phone/James/phone him now/No
6. forget/cassettes/go and get them/Yes

3. Comment on suggestions

What's that noise? Is it a car?
No, it can't be a car. It's too loud.
Is it a motorbike?
It might be a motorbike. It sounds like one.

1. car/can't be/too loud
2. motorbike/might be/sounds like one
3. lorry/is/see it now
4. television/can't be/turned off
5. radio/might be/sounds like it
6. Peter/is/I can see him now

4. Answer the questions about when things happened

When were X-Rays invented?
They were invented in 1895.
When was oxygen discovered?
It was discovered in 1774.

1. X-Rays/invent/1895
2. oxygen/discover/1774
3. radium/discover/1898
4. aeroplane/invent/1903
5. long-playing record/invent/1948
6. Nazca lines/discover/1939

5. Talk about yourself

(Open exercise)
When were you born?
(I was born in 1976.)

1. When were you born?
2. Where were you born?
3. When did you first go to school?
4. Where was your first school?
5. What was the first film you went to see?
6. How old were you when you went to see it?

LESSONS 46-50

1. Agree with people's wishes

I'd like to live in Canada.
Yes, I wish I lived in Canada.
I'd like to speak several languages.
Yes, I wish I spoke several languages.

1. live in Canada
2. speak several languages
3. have a lot of money
4. have a job
5. be able to drive
6. have a bigger bedroom

2. Express regrets

Does he live in your street?
Yes, I wish he didn't live in my street.
Does he go to your school?
Yes, I wish he didn't go to my school.

1. live in my street
2. go to my school
3. go to school on the same bus
4. wait for me after school
5. walk home with me

3. Give advice

Shall I take a bus to the match or walk?
If I were you, I'd walk.

1. take a bus to the match/walk
2. take £5/£10
3. get my ticket at the door/buy one now
4. buy lunch there/take sandwiches
5. wear my new trousers/my old jeans

4. Respond to suggestions

Let's have a fashion page.

That's a good idea. We could have a fashion page.

And how about a problem page?

Not really. I don't think we ought to have a problem page.

Suggestions

1. fashion page ✓
2. problem page ✗
3. sports page ✓
4. children's page ✗
5. music page ✓
6. page of
   short stories ✗

5. Talk about you

(Open exercise)

How long have you been studying English?

(About three years.)

1. How long have you been studying English?
2. Do you think it's difficult or easy?
3. What do you want to do when you leave school?
4. Will English help you to do this?
5. What is the most difficult thing about learning English?
6. Do you think you will ever speak perfect English?

Words and expressions

LESSON 1

ambition
chess
computer studies
examination
famine relief
fashion design
guitar
poetry
politician

admire
cycle
raise (money)

important
spare
special

someone

in two years' time

LESSON 2

journey
rucksack
term

bother
need(n't)

round

You are lucky!
a couple of months

LESSON 3

accident
bone
event
experience
tonne (ton)
tournament

break
fall off

foreign

once
twice

LESSON 4

argument
driver
lift

allow
attack
forbid
hitch-hike

murder
rob

dangerous
friendly
present
scruffy

at once
nowadays

for
since

LESSON 5

hovercraft
present

get off
pass (exam)

by chance

LESSON 6

album
company
director
hippopotamus
magazine
office
petrol station
purse
staff
ticket inspector

extra
latest (= most recent)
part-time

already
just
still
yet

I'm afraid.
That's a shame.
You are a pain!

LESSON 7

motorway
route
signpost
tram
turning

enclose
reach
turn off

along
down

How often?

LESSON 8

amazement

accept
answer
begin
bet
continue
lose
reply

LESSON 9

basket
century
crew
duck
freedom
gas burner
gliding
ground
hang-gliding
hot-air balloon
passenger
pilot
sheep
skating
wing

consist
discover
float
land

You can't fool me!
quite honestly

LESSON 10

alarm clock
bath
coalminer
farmer
ice skating
lot
person
scientist
soldier
splash

book
cure
defend
dig
draw
grow

hire
persuade
produce
receive
rule
sink
splash

LESSON 11

building site
harbour
Old People's Home
relation
wreck

cheer
have a look
inspect

nearly
suddenly

somebody

Guess who…?
Really!
What on earth…?

LESSON 12

adventure
autumn
clothes
collar
old-fashioned
rose
stone seat

dream

following

strangely

as
while

LESSON 13

citizen
drop
jewel
ruby
sapphire
statue
swallow
sword
tears

cover
cry
fly
pour

run down

miserable

LESSON 14

actress
agent
eyebrows
hairstyle
part (in film)
pudding
role
sense of humour

behead
look
smell
sound
taste

confident
delicious
leading

on location

LESSON 15

forest
police officer
robber

pull

world-famous

tightly

LESSON 16

autograph
cafeteria
captivity
dolphin
killer whale
licensed bar
parrot
reserve
sea lion

feed
roam

cruel
daily

LESSON 17

church
dentist
gym class
health
human
hygiene

blink

approximately
on average

LESSON 18

channel
comedy
crime series
documentary
nature programme
quiz programme
soap opera
survey
total
variety show

broadcast

popular

recent

LESSON 19

entertainer
habitat
human being
lifespan
mammal
myth
pool
space
species
sunglasses
trick
trumpet

blow
perform
shorten
survive
commercial

healthy
intelligent

although
basically
however
rarely

sense of fun

LESSON 20

stage

relax

fluently

LESSON 21

athlete
bronze
character
dentist
drill
filling
injection
medal

break
burn
fall over
hurt
knock over

afterwards
definitely
possibly
wide

I'm afraid
Be careful!

LESSON 22

brickyard
cap
communication
disease
eel
family life
horse-drawn coach
leisure
pie
seaside
servant
swimmer
taste
transport
twopence

poor
slum

LESSON 23

button
doorbell
message
parcel
push button
thing
tool box

call
check
connect
explain
hesitate
point
press

square
valuable

politely
puzzled

someone
somewhere

LESSON 24

acid
adult
boiled sweet
braces
chewing-gum
decay (tooth)
false teeth
fizzy-drink
ice-lolly
metal
peanut
smile
toffee

boast
cause
rot
stare

ugly

surprisingly

I can't stand…

LESSON 25

accident
childhood
midnight
pocket money

perfectly

Don't be silly.

LESSON 26

diary
game
object
score
spaceship

change (money)
give back
miss

man-made
outer

be in trouble
Hang on.
Leave them alone.
Let's get out of here.
Shut up!
you lot
What's going on?
You're nothing but
    trouble.

LESSON 27

bottom
captain
creature
enemy
instruction manual
laser gun
planet
satellite
S.O.S.

capture
crash
escape
explode
fight
float
shoot

digital
flesh-eating

on fire

everywhere

LESSON 28

fit
performance
superstar

annoy
behave
criticise
praise
train

sensible

regularly

LESSON 29

archer
astronomer
atom
balance
bull
cloud
constellation
crab
dense
dwarf
galaxy
giant
goat
hydrogen gas
pattern
plough
ram
reptile
scorpion
soil
star
temperature
virgin
water carrier
zodiac

depend
gaze
vary

brightly
dim

closely

LESSON 30

finger
palm
palmistry
personality
shape
talent
texture

develop
indicate

even-tempered
methodical
nervous
talented

LESSON 31

barbecue
detail
gala
gran
granny
mirror
patience
shelter
skill
tent
violin

amuse
cheer up
confirm
occupy

depressed
survival

yourself/ves

Don't worry.

LESSON 32

bamboo
coconut
desert island
fishing rod
lagoon
pipe
plenty
shell
storm
thirst

manage
rescue
row
tour

shipwrecked
single-handed

ever since
fortunately

LESSON 33

act
body
companion
courage

death
end
expedition
heart
hope
noon
sleeping bag
snowstorm
thought

complete
hope

brave
worse

surely

LESSON 34

ankle
block
blubber
bridge
dog team
edge
fridge
husky dog
hut
igloo
inhabitant
pile
skin
sled
snow
steel
surface
terrain
territory
trail

deserve
hug
hunt
protect
situate
wrap

bitter
punishing
smelly
smoky
tough
wild-eyed

above
across
ahead
among
around
below
over
through

LESSON 35

archway
arrow
castle
hill
hut
leader
parade
river bank
wedding

LESSON 36

bar
cash box
cloakroom
costume
cotton
eyepatch
flour
leather
nylon
omelette
pirate
plastic
safe
screen
smuggler
wool

mark
store
type

gigantic
terrific
top

LESSON 37

anatomy
check-in desk
kiosk
lecture
lecturer
neighbour
skeleton

pack
wonder

LESSON 38

barrel
bay
candle
goods
graveyard
hole

inn
passage
shadow
shore
signal
stone
storeroom

explore
hold

asleep
secret
still

except

LESSON 39

amplifier
backing group
business
cave
charts
docks
failure
loudspeaker
microphone
orchestra
pony
pop video
setting
warehouse

disappear
include
promote
set

conceptual
empty
exotic
several
tropical

therefore

where

at the moment
the bit…

LESSON 40

amazement
audience
mattress
screen
studio
taxi fare
waistcoat
wall

attach
film
fix
pay
place
project
report
support
yawn

horizontal

in case

LESSON 41

puncture

get into trouble
get the sack
had better
knock over
oversleep

sour
suspicious

by accident
instead
urgently

Hi folks!
Watch it!

LESSON 42

bulb
detective
postmark
shape
tulip bulb
weather forecast
whistle

plant

probably

on the other hand

LESSON 43

adaptor
appointment
bow tie
detective
dollar bill
electric razor
eyesight
felt tip pen
optician
spectacle case

investigate
mend

stare
trace

attractive
elementary
old-fashioned
rude

rather
unusually

LESSON 44

area
atom bomb
base
battle
desert
pilot
position
runway
spacecraft
theory
tomb

invent
launch
remain

accurate
alien
astonishing
geometric
huge
mysterious
prehistoric
straight

LESSON 45

archaeologist
coast guard
expert
government
press conference
reward
treasure
wreck

consist of
scuba dive
sink

worth
startling

officially

LESSON 46

birthmark

avoid
go out with somebody
take notice
wish

Worse luck!

LESSON 47

martial arts

fed up
fun
lonely
miserable

Never mind!

LESSON 48

fear
feather
goose
hunchback
lighthouse
mouth (of river)

push
remind

gentle
romantic
rough

LESSON 49

advice
career
cartoon
competition
cookery
editor
fashion
feature
free offer

gossip
hairdo
make-up
model
review
tip

fabulous
sensational

LESSON 50

barometer
cot
customer
size
tractor

existing

Common irregular verbs

These verbs are in their infinitive/past tense/past participle forms.

VERBS WITH NO CHANGE

cost	cost	cost
cut	cut	cut
hit	hit	hit
hurt	hurt	hurt
let	let	let
put	put	put
set	set	set
shut	shut	shut

VERBS WITH ONE CHANGE

babysit	babysat	babysat
bring	brought	brought
build	built	built
burn	burned/	burned/
	burnt	burnt
buy	bought	bought
catch	caught	caught
dig	dug	dug
dream	dreamed/	dreamed/
	dreamt	dreamt
feed	fed	fed
feel	felt	felt
fight	fought	fought
find	found	found
get	got	got
hang	hung	hung
have	had	had
hear	heard	heard
hold	held	held
keep	kept	kept
learn	learnt	learnt
leave	left	left
lend	lent	lent
lose	lost	lost
make	made	made
mean	meant	meant
meet	met	met
oversleep	overslept	overslept
pay	paid	paid
read	read	read
say	said	said
sell	sold	sold
send	sent	sent
shine	shone	shone
sit	sat	sat
sleep	slept	slept
spell	spelled/	spelled/
	spelt	spelt
spend	spent	spent
stand	stood	stood
tell	told	told
think	thought	thought
understand	understood	understood
win	won	won

VERBS WITH TWO CHANGES

be	was	been
begin	began	begun
blow	blew	blown
break	broke	broken
choose	chose	chosen
come	came	come
do	did	done
draw	drew	drawn
drink	drank	drunk
drive	drove	driven
eat	ate	eaten
fall	fell	fallen
fly	flew	flown
forbid	forbade	forbidden
forget	forgot	forgotten
give	gave	given
go	went	gone
grow	grew	grown
know	knew	known
lie	lay	lain
ride	rode	ridden
ring	rang	rung
run	ran	run
see	saw	seen
show	showed	shown
sing	sang	sung
sink	sank	sunk
speak	spoke	spoken
steal	stole	stolen
swim	swam	swum
take	took	taken
tear	tore	torn
throw	threw	thrown
wear	wore	worn
write	wrote	written

The following extracts are taken from Longman readers:

Page 12: Round the World in Eighty Days (LSR Stage 3)
Page 20: The Young King and other stories (NMSR Stage 3)
Page 36: 2001 and Beyond: Science Fiction Stories (LSES)
Page 52: Race to the South Pole (LSR Stage 4)
Page 60: Moonfleet (NMSR Stage 3)
Page 68: The Return of Sherlock Holmes (NMSR Stage 3)
Page 76: The Snow Goose and other stories (NMSR Stage 3)

For details of Longman's complete range of readers, contact your local Longman office or write direct to:

The Promotions Department
English Language Teaching Division
Longman House
Burnt Mill
Harlow
Essex
CM20 2JE

Longman Group UK Limited
Longman House, Burnt Mill, Harlow,
Essex CM20 2JE, England
and Associated Companies throughout the world.

First published 1987
Eighteenth impression 1995

ISBN 0-582-51434-7

Designed by Nucleus Design Associates

Illustrated by Chris Ryley
with Andrew Aloof, Trevor Parkin, Jane Lydbury, Val Hill, Steve Kyte,
Mark Peppé, Andrew Tudor, Hardlines

Set in Scantext Palatino
Printed in Italy by G. Canale & C. S.p.A. Borgaro T.se - Turin
NPC/15

Acknowledgements

We are grateful to the following for permission to reproduce copyright photographs:

Ace Photo Agency for page 38 (bottom right); All-Sport (UK) Ltd for page 27 (inset); Art Directors Photo Library for pages 5 (bottom) & 31 (inset); BBC Hulton Picture Library for page 35 (top middle); Heather Angel/Biofotos for page 29-30 (Background); Britain On View (BTA/ETB) for page 25 (bottom); Bruce Coleman Ltd for page 30 (inset); Camera Press Ltd for pages 18 (bottom left) & 35 (bottom middle); The J. Allan Cash Photolibrary for pages 13, 15 (right) & 67; Camouflage Concerts Ltd for page 39 (right); The Cavalry and Guards Club for page 52; Frank Hermann/Colorific for page 1-2 (main picture); Brigitte Lacombe/Colorific for page 1 (top); Duncan Raban/Colorific for page 2 (top); David Turnley/Colorific for page 2 (Bottom); Fjallraven Ltd for page 49; Geoff Howard for page 77-78 (main picture); Howarth-Loomes Collection for page 35 (right); Impact Photos for page 61-62 (bottom); Longman Group UK Ltd/photo by Alyson Lee for page 14; Longman Group UK Ltd/photo by Pentaprism for page 55; Longman Photographic Unit for pages 5-6 (main picture), 5 (top), 11, 27, 31, 37 (top), 37 (bottom right), 39 (left), 44 & 79-80; Mecca Leisure Ltd for page 15 (left); The World Atlas of Mysteries by Francis Hitching/Pan Books Ltd for page 69-70 (main picture), Photo Library International-Leeds for pages 6 (top) & 38 (top middle); Pictor International-London for pages 2 (middle right) & 38 (bottom left); Picturepoint-London for pages 6 (bottom), 29 (inset) & 71; Popperfoto for page 54; Radio Times for page 28; RETNA Pictures Ltd for page 61-62 (inset); Picture courtesy of ROOT Magazine for page 77 (bottom); Scope Features for page 21-22; Tony Morrison/South American Pictures for page 69 (inset); Sporting Pictures (UK) Ltd for page 2 (middle left); Susan Griggs Agency Ltd for page 69-70 (inset); Syndication International Library for pages 1 (bottom) & 18 (top right); Tim Graham Picture Library for page 18 (top left) & (bottom right); Topham Picture Library for pages 4 & 26 (right); J. Bond/ Transworld Features for page 28 (inset); University College Hospital for page 38 (top left) & (top right); Videoweek for page 61 (bottom); Windsor Safari Park for pages 25 (top) & 26 (top left) & (bottom left); Woodmansterne/R. Warner for page 7; Zefa for page 45.

We have been unable to trace the copyright holders of the photographs on pages 35 (left) & 37 (bottom left) and would be grateful for any information that would enable us to do so.

We are grateful to the following for permission to reproduce copyright material:

Associated Newspapers Group plc for an adapted extract from the article 'The woman who won man's toughest race' by Douglas Thompson from p15 *Daily Mail* (22/3/85).

We are grateful for the information which has been used from the following publications:

The Complete Traveller by Joan Bakewell, published by Sidgwick and Jackson (page 5), *Junior Education Special Number 12* published by Scholastic Publications (magazine) (page 13), *Games for Language Learning* by Andrew Wright, published by Cambridge University Press (page 47).

The text on page 21 is based on facts in an article in *You, The Mail on Sunday Magazine*.

Aprobado por el Ministerio de
Educación y Ciencia con
fecha 17 de marzo de 1988.